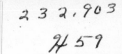
Jesus, The New Elijah

Paul Hinnebusch, O.P.

Servant Books
Ann Arbor, Michigan

97-916

ACKNOWLEDGEMENTS AND BIBLIOGRAPHY

Much of our explanation of the Scriptures concerning Elijah as a prefiguring of Jesus depends upon a very literal translation which keeps the Jewish idioms. Contemporary translations of the Scriptures tend to paraphrase these idioms, and therefore some of the meaning is lost. In many cases, therefore, we have had to use old translations, such as the Douay-Rheims and the Confraternity of Christian Doctrine Version.

The following symbols after the scriptural references indicate the versions used:

a — *The Anchor Bible*, copyright 1966 by Doubleday and Company, Inc.

b — The latest edition of *La Bible de Jerusalem* (Paris, 1973).

c — *The Holy Bible*, copyright 1962 by the Confraternity of Christian Doctrine.

d — Douay-Rheims.

e — *The New English Bible*, copyright 1970 by The Delegates of the Oxford University Press and the Syndics of the Cambridge University Press.

g — *The Grail Psalter*, copyright 1963, by The Grail, England.

j — *The Jerusalem Bible*, copyright 1966 by Doubleday and Company, Inc.

m — *Modern Language Bible*, copyright 1969, Zondervan Publishing House.

n — *The New American Bible*, copyright 1970 by the Confraternity of Christian Doctrine.

r — *Revised Standard Version*, copyright 1946 & 1952 by the Division of Christian Education of the National Council of the Churches of Christ in the U.S.A.

We are also greatly indebted to the following works which we used in our studies in preparing this book:

Gerhard von Rad, *Old Testament Theology*, Vol. II (New York: Harper & Row, 1962), p. 14-32.

Jean Steinmann, *Le Prophétisme Biblique des Origines a Osée* (Paris: du Cerf, 1959), p. 85-117.

Roland E. Murphy, "Élie," *Dictionnaire de Spiritualité*, Vol. IV (Paris, 1959), columns 565-67.

Louis Bouyer, *The Meaning of Sacred Scripture* (Notre Dame, 1958), p. 149-155.

The Jerome Biblical Commentary, on pertinent passages in Luke, Mark, and the Book of Kings.

CONTENTS

Introduction / 1

1. *Elijah's Assumption* / 5
   "If You See Me Taken Up" (2 Kings 2:10) / 5
   Elijah Taken Up / 6
   "A Double Portion of Your Spirit" (2 Kings 2:9) / 7
   "Clothed with Power from on High" (Luke 24:49) / 9
   "Messengers before His Face" (Luke 9:52) / 10
   "As Yahweh Lives and as You Live" (2 Kings 2:2) / 13

2. *Elijah: Yahweh's Servant* / 15
   "Before Whom I Stand" (1 Kings 17:1) / 15
   "Yahweh Lives!" (2 Kings 2:2) / 17
   "He Gave Him Back to His Mother" (1 Kings 17:23;
      Luke 7:15) / 20

3. *Elijah Moved by the Spirit* / 23
   "The Spirit of the Lord Will Carry You"
      (1 Kings 18:12) / 23
   Yahweh's Fiery Chariot (Ezekiel 1 & 10) / 24
   "Jesus, Full of the Spirit" (Luke 4:1) / 26

4. *Elijah's Wholeheartedness* / 29
   My God Is Yahweh! / 29
   Yahweh's Holy War / 31
   Elijah's Intercession on Mount Carmel / 34
   My God Is Jesus! / 35

5. *Elijah Discouraged* / 39
   "Only a Man Like Us" (James 5:17) / 39
   "The Lord Will Be Passing By" (1 Kings 19:11) / 42
   "The Sound of a Gentle Breeze" (1 Kings 19:12) / 43

6. *Elijah's Intercession on Mount Horeb* / 45
    "What Are You Doing Here, Elijah?"
        (1 Kings 19:9) / 45
    Fire and Sword / 47
    "Hear Me, O Lord!" (1 Kings 18:37) / 49
    Courage in Our Mission / 50

7. *Elijah's Heavenly Intercession* / 51
    "An Angel Appeared to Strengthen Him"
        (Luke 22:39-46) / 51
    "I Alone Am Left" (1 Kings 19:10) / 52
    "Sorrowful Even to Death" (Mark 14:34) / 53
    "The Fervent Petition of a Holy Man" (James 5:16) / 54
    "He Blessed Them" (Luke 24:50) / 56

8. *Eucharistic Intercession* / 59
    Priestly Intercession / 60
    Christian Intercession / 61

9. *The Spirit and Power of Elijah* / 65
    "I Have Come to Cast Fire" (Luke 12:49) / 67
    The Spirit of Jesus / 69

10. *Jesus and Elisha's Vocation* / 75
    First Vocation Story:
        "Nowhere to Lay His Head" (Luke 9:58) / 76
    Second Vocation Story:
        "Let the Dead Bury Their Dead" (Luke 9:60) / 79
    Third Vocation Story:
        "Let Me Take Leave of My People" (Luke 9:61) / 81

11. *Elijah's Mantle* / 85
    "Elijah Cast His Mantle upon Him" (1 Kings 19:9) / 85
    "I Spread My Cloak over You" (Ezekiel 16:8) / 87
    "Clothed with Power from on High" (Luke 24:49) / 88

12. *Jesus and the Holy War* / 91
    "I Have Married a Wife" (Luke 14:20) / 93
    Was Elijah a Celibate? / 94

13. *Elijah, the Precursor* / 97
   "I Send My Messenger" (Matthew 11:20) / 97
   Precursor of the Day of the Lord (Malachi 3:28) / 98
   "The Messenger of the Covenant" (Malachi 3:1) / 100
   Luke and Malachi / 103
   The Lord's Presentation in the Temple (Luke 2:22) / 105
   The Cleansing of the Temple (Luke 19:45-48) / 106

14. *Jesus, the Precursor* / 107
   "Elijah Will Restore Everything" (Mark 9:12) / 107
   Precursor into Heaven (Hebrews 6:19-20) / 109
   "Two and Two before His Face" (Luke 10:1) / 109
   The Two Witnesses (Revelation 11:3-13) / 110

15. *See Elijah and Live!* / 113
   "We Too Shall Have Life!" (Sirach 48:11) / 113
   Simeon Sees the Lord's Anointed (Luke 2:25-35) / 118
   "Will Not Taste Death" (Luke 9:27) / 120
   "A Hard Saying" (John 6:60) / 121
   "Lord, That I May See!" (Luke 18:41) / 123

16. *What They Saw on Calvary* / 125
   The Cross and the Conversion of Hearts / 127
   Seeing the "Just Man" (Luke 23:47) / 130

INTRODUCTION

But the angel said to him, "Do not be afraid, Zechariah, for your prayer is heard, and your wife Elizabeth will bear you a son, and you shall call his name John. . . . He will be filled with the Holy Spirit, even from his mother's womb. . . . And he will go before the Lord in the spirit and power of Elijah . . . to make ready for the Lord a people prepared (Luke 1:13-17,*r*).

Every Christian is called to be another John the Baptist, to go before the Lord in the spirit and power of Elijah—not the old Elijah, but Jesus, the New Elijah.

St. Luke presents Jesus as the New Elijah. Under the guidance of Luke, we shall examine the story of the Old Elijah to discover what the Spirit and power of the New Elijah is, and what it means for us to go before the Lord Jesus in his Spirit and power.

In presenting Jesus as the New Elijah, St. Luke in no way contradicts Jesus, who said that John the Baptist is "Elijah who is to come" (Matt. 17:13). The figure of Elijah is a fitting image for expressing aspects both of Jesus and of John. Just as John the Baptist's mission can be better understood with the help of the Elijah imagery, so too can the mission of Jesus. In fact, St. Luke sees a more perfect similarity to Elijah in Jesus than in John the Baptist. This will become clear in the course of this book.

Why Such a Book?

Luke's presentation of Jesus as the New Elijah is an excellent example of typology. Typology is the use of Old Testament figures to express New Testament realities. Thus, St. Paul tells us that "Adam was a type of the one who was to

1

come" (Rom. 5:14). He contrasts the first Adam with Jesus, "the last Adam" (1 Cor. 15:45-49). He expresses Christian baptism in terms of Israel's passage through the Red Sea (1 Cor. 10:1-2), and the Eucharist in terms of the manna and the water from the rock (1 Cor. 10:3-4). The rock is a type of Christ (10:4).

By using types from the Old Testament, the New Testament authors express spiritual realities in striking imagery which captures the imagination and draws the heart. That is our purpose in this book. In presenting Jesus as the New Elijah, we try to bring out in a striking way what Jesus is for us. He is our precursor into heaven, taken up to God as Elijah was, clothing us with his own spirit and power, and sending us forth on his own mission. We hope that each of our readers will be able to see himself in Elijah and in Jesus, and will be moved to live the Christian realities expressed in these figures.

The book is intended for all of God's people, but it also has many passages valuable for the personal lives of priests. These same passages are valuable for the laity as well, since they give insight into the priesthood of all the faithful.

The detailed table of contents and the index at the end of the book are intended to make the book useful as a guide in Scripture study and discussion. Some of the Scripture passages are taken up more than once in the book; the various references can be tracked down in the index. In that way, special themes can be singled out from the book for further reflection, and the reader can quickly look up an earlier treatment of a passage when it comes up again for further consideration.

The book is more homiletical than exegetical, for it endeavors to bring out the meaning of the Scriptures for present day readers. It has its origins in a retreat preached by the author. During the week of the retreat, the daily Scripture readings in the Sacred Liturgy were the story of Elijah from the Books of Kings (Tenth Week of Ordinary Time, Year II). Jesus, the New Elijah, became the focus of the whole retreat. At a later date, the ideas of the retreat were expanded in ten classroom lectures, in which all the passages of the Scriptures dealing with Elijah were treated. Therefore to some extent the exegetical quality has also come into the book.

The book's frequent references to the Eucharist and to the priesthood of Christ are due to the fact that much of the book was originally homilies preached during the retreat. For this reason, too, Elijah emerges in the book as a man of prayer and a great intercessor, prefiguring Jesus, "our precursor who has entered on our behalf" into heaven (Heb. 6:20), where he "forever lives to make intercession" (Heb. 7:25). As new Elijahs, we too are called by the Lord to join him in his own intercession. Zechariah's words to his son, John the Baptist, can be truthfully addressed to each one of us as we accept our Christian mission:

And you, O child, shall be called prophet of the Most High; for you shall go before the Lord to prepare straight paths for him, giving his people a knowledge of salvation, in freedom from their sins (Luke 1:76-77,*n*).

CHAPTER ONE

ELIJAH'S ASSUMPTION

"If You See Me Taken Up"

Elijah said to Elisha, "Ask for whatever I may do for you, before I am taken from you." Elisha answered, "May I receive a double portion of your spirit." "You have asked something that is not easy," he replied. "Still, if you see me taken up from you, your wish will be granted; otherwise not." As they walked on conversing, a flaming chariot and flaming horses came between them, and Elijah went up to heaven in a whirlwind. When Elisha saw it happen he cried, "My father! my father! Israel's chariots and drivers!" But when he could no longer see him, Elisha gripped his own garment and tore it in two (2 Kings 2:9-12,*n*).

In presenting Jesus as the new Elijah, Luke's Gospel refers back to this account of Elijah's assumption. Luke frames the whole story of the Lord's journey up to Jerusalem to die between two statements about his being "taken up":

When the days had come for him to be *taken up*, he steadfastly set his face to go to Jerusalem (Luke 9:51,*c*, emphasis added).

He led them out near Bethany, and with hands upraised, blessed them. As he blessed, he left them, and was *taken up* to heaven (Luke 24:50-51,*n*, emphasis added).

Luke is using the literary device of inclusion. Everything within an inclusion is to be interpreted in the light of the opening and closing statements. In this case, the term "taken up" is the clue to our understanding of the Lord's great pilgrimage up to Jerusalem where he is to suffer and die.

In the first statement, "he set his face" is a Semitic idiom meaning "to face opposition and hostility courageously." "He steadfastly set his face to go to Jerusalem" tells us not only the direction Jesus took, but also the nature of his journey. His life is an ascension, through hostility and death, to the fullness of glory. "Was it not necessary that the Christ should suffer these things and enter into his glory?" (Luke 24:26,r). The Lord's whole journey up to Jerusalem and his crucifixion there are but one movement into glory. His pilgrimage to Jerusalem and his death on the cross is really his journey to his Father's house.

This journey is foreshadowed in Luke's story of Jesus at the age of twelve going up to Jerusalem with his parents on a religious pilgrimage at the Feast of Passover. When his parents find him in the temple after a three days' search, he says to them, "Did you not know that I had to be in my Father's house?" (Luke 2:49,n). This story is a tableau which depicts the whole life of Jesus as a passover pilgrimage, a going home to his Father in heaven.

If we examine the whole story of Elijah's assumption (2 Kings 2:1-18), we will find that it has something to say to us about our Lord's pilgrimage.

Elijah Taken Up

The prophet Elijah had once made a pilgrimage to a mountain top, and there he met with God (1 Kings 19:1-18). Later, he was "taken up" in the fiery chariot, to be with God permanently. As the delightful story about his being taken up begins (2 Kings 2:1-15), the prophet seems to know that his life on earth is at an end. He tries to break away from his faithful servant Elisha. "Stay here at Gilgal, please," he tells him. "The Lord has sent me to Bethel." Elijah wants to be alone, so that he can meet God with full attention. He craves solitude, so that he can prepare in prayer to meet his Lord.

But Elisha will give him no peace. He keeps tagging along after Elijah, who cannot shake him loose. To Elijah's request that he stay at Gilgal, Elisha answers, "As the Lord lives, and as you yourself live, I will not leave you." So off they go to Bethel, where the conversation is repeated. "Stay here, please, for the Lord has sent me on to Jericho." Again Elisha swears by God's life, and by Elijah's life with God, that he will not leave him. Off they go to Jericho. Elijah says to Elisha, "Please stay here, for the Lord has sent me on to the Jordan." And Elisha again repeats his oath of faithfulness.

Does he have something more in mind than dogged faithfulness to his leader? He knows that something is about to happen. He knows that Elijah is going to be taken from him, and he wants to be with him till the last precious moment. Friendship with Elijah is precious indeed, and Elisha wants to profit from it to the very end. "Blessed are they that saw thee, and were honored with thy friendship" (Sir. 48:11,d).

As Elisha follows Elijah from place to place on this last journey, the brotherhoods of prophets come out everywhere to meet them, and everywhere they annoy Elisha with that word, "taken up." "Do you know that the Lord will take your master from over you today?" "Yes, I know it," he replies each time; "Keep still!"

"A Double Portion of Your Spirit"

When Elijah sees that he cannot shake off his faithful disciple and friend, he says to him, "Ask for whatever I may do for you, before I am taken from you." Elisha answers, "May I receive a double portion of your spirit" (2 Kings 2:9,n).

It was customary in Israel for the elder son to receive a double portion of the father's heritage and to become the father of the clan in his father's place, the leader of all the families descended from his father (Deut. 21:17). In asking for a double portion of Elijah's prophetic spirit, Elisha wishes to be acknowledged as Elijah's spiritual heir, and therefore the leader and father of the whole brotherhood of prophets. This brotherhood had been calling Elijah "Father." Elisha himself, when he sees Elijah taken up in the chariot, cries out, "My father, my father!" (2 Kings 2:12).

Elisha is asking, then, to be head prophet to succeed Elijah. To this request, Elijah replies, "You have asked a hard thing" (2 Kings 2:10,n). It is a hard request, because the prophetic spirit is not passed on by inheritance, nor can anyone transfer it to someone else. It comes from God alone, who gives it to whomever he chooses.

Elijah cannot bestow his prophetic spirit upon Elisha, but he implies that he will intercede with Yahweh on Elisha's behalf. For he gives Elisha a sign by which he will know whether Yahweh, the giver of the spirit, has granted his request: "Still, if you *see* me taken up from you, your wish will be granted; otherwise not" (2 Kings 2:10,n).

Elisha *saw* him taken up! This was the sign that he truly was God's chosen successor to Elijah. Elisha takes up Elijah's mantle. The mantle is the symbol of Elijah's spirit and authority with which Elisha is now clothed.

After Elijah is taken up, leaving his mantle behind for Elisha, the brotherhood of prophets acknowledges that this has happened. When they see Elisha repeat Elijah's miracle of dividing the waters of the Jordan with Elijah's mantle, they say, "The spirit of Elijah rests on Elisha" (2 Kings 2:15,n). They go to meet him, and bow to the ground before him. By this sign of reverence, they acknowledge his authority over them. And at once, in a practical way, they prove their acceptance of his authority by asking his permission for something they want to do. They want to send fifty of their number to search for Elijah.

Elisha knows that what they request is futile, but like every good father, he knows that he has to let them learn the hard way. Experience is the best teacher, but the tuition is so high! If only we would accept the word of authority in trusting obedience.

Elisha indeed becomes the father of a family of prophets. In the stories which follow in the Elisha cycle, we see how the company of prophets lives a community life with Elisha. Together they build a larger house to live in (2 Kings 6:1-7), together they eat the vegetable stew prepared by Elisha's servant (2 Kings 4:38-41), together they are nourished by the barley loaves multiplied by Elisha, foreshadowing the multiplication of loaves by Jesus (2 Kings 4:42-44).

"Clothed with Power from on High"

Just before Jesus was taken up, he said to his disciples, "Remain here in the city until you are clothed with power from on high" (Luke 24:49,*n*). They are to wear the Lord's own mantle of authority. They are to be clothed with the promised Holy Spirit. "See, I send down upon you the promise of my Father" (Luke 24:49,*n*).

Luke tells us that the disciples saw Jesus taken up, just as Elisha saw Elijah taken up. "He was lifted up before their eyes" (Acts 1:9,*n*). This seeing is the sign that they will be clothed with the Holy Spirit, and endowed with the Lord's power to continue his mission, just as Elisha had continued the work of Elijah.

> You will receive power when the Holy Spirit comes down on you. Then you are to be my witnesses in Jerusalem, throughout Judea and Samaria, yes, even to the ends of the earth. No sooner had he said this than he was lifted up before their eyes *in a cloud* which took him from their sight (Acts 1:8-9,*n*, emphasis added).

In the Old Testament, God's chariot was a cloud. "You make the clouds your chariot; you travel on the wings of the wind" (Ps. 104:3,*n*). "See, the Lord is riding on a swift cloud on his way to Egypt!" (Isa. 19:1,*n*). The chariot of fire on which Elijah was taken up has been compared by the Jewish rabbis with the fiery chariot on which the divine Presence was enthroned in Ezekiel's vision (Ezek. 1 & 10). Like Elijah, Jesus is taken up in God's own chariot to where God is enthroned above the cherubim.

Seeing him taken up, the disciples are assured that they will be his spiritual heirs, endowed with his own Spirit and power.

"Messengers before His Face"

It was not just the eleven apostles who were clothed with the Lord's Spirit and power, to be new Elijahs preparing the Lord's way. After the Lord's ascension, "about a hundred and twenty" (Acts 1:15,*r*) were persevering in prayer with one accord, with Mary, the Mother of Jesus, awaiting the coming of the promised Spirit (Acts 1:13-14). "They were all together in one place" (Acts 2:1,*r*), and "they were *all* filled with the Holy Spirit" (Acts 2:4,*r*, emphasis added).

These one hundred and twenty were the whole Church at that time; they were all the believers in the risen Lord. They were "the first fruits" of the New Israel, and therefore in their persons they represented the whole Christian Church of all times and places. Thus they were indeed the whole people of God, gathered together with Mary, waiting for "the promise of my Father" (Luke 24:49,*n*). When the Promise was sent, "they were all filled with the Holy Spirit" (Acts 2:4), all were "clothed with power from on high" (Luke 24:49,*n*).

Thus all of God's people received the mantle of Jesus, the New Elijah, all were commissioned to share in the Lord's own mission. That this is Luke's thinking is evident, furthermore, when he describes how Jesus sent out the seventy-two disciples in addition to the twelve apostles: "And after these things, the Lord appointed also other seventy-two, and he sent them two and two *before his face* into every city and place whither he himself was to come" (Luke 10:1,*d*, emphasis added). The seventy-two, which can be treated as seventy for the purposes of this discussion, are symbolic of all Christians. And the phrase Luke applies to them—"before his face"—is another reference to Elijah.

Earlier in Luke's gospel, Gabriel uses this phrase in announcing the birth of John the Baptist: "He will be filled with the Holy Spirit even from his mother's womb. . . . And he will go *before the Lord* in the spirit and power of Elijah . . . to make ready for the Lord a people prepared" (Luke 1:15, 17,*r*, emphasis added here and in following quotations). The phrase refers to the prophecy of Malachi, which foretold Elijah's return to prepare for the Lord's coming: "Behold I send my [messenger], and he shall prepare the way *before my face*" (Mal. 3:1,*d*).

After the death of John the Baptist, when Jesus set out on his last journey to Jerusalem, "he sent messengers *before his face* ... to prepare for him" (Luke 9:52,*d*). "And after these things, the Lord appointed also other seventy-two, and he sent them two and two *before his face* into every city and place whither he himself was to come" (Luke 10:1,*d*).

"Before his face" is an expression denoting a theophany—a manifestation of God. Malachi is telling us that God will manifest his face, that he will show his presence and power. The mission of the seventy disciples is to prepare the way for the coming of the Lord in person; he will manifest his presence to those who are prepared to receive him.

Every Christian disciple is sent "before his face" as another Elijah; for those seventy sent by the Lord to prepare the way before him are symbolic of all Christians. To fully understand this symbolism, we must look to a story in the book of Numbers that tells how seventy elders of the Israelites were given a share in the prophetic spirit of Moses.

When the Israelites were in the Sinai, Moses complained to God about the excessive burden they had become to him. God told him to call together seventy elders, and said, "I will take some of the spirit which is upon you, and put it upon them" (Num. 11:17,*r*). Two of the elders did not come to the assembly at the Lord's meeting tent, but remained in the camp. And yet the spirit of God came upon them, too, and they prophesied (Num. 11:26).

Joshua, "who from his youth had been Moses' aide" (Num. 11:28,*n*), seemed to be jealous of the new recipients of the Spirit, and said, "My lord Moses, forbid them" (11:28). But Moses said to him, "Are you jealous for my sake? Would that all the Lord's people were prophets, that the Lord would put his Spirit upon them!" (Num. 11:29,*r*).

Moses desired that all of God's people would receive the Holy Spirit. His prayer was finally answered on Pentecost when Jesus, who had ascended to the Father, poured out the Holy Spirit upon all the disciples. Peter stood up on that occasion, and explained that thus was fulfilled the prophecy of Joel, who said that in the last days the Holy Spirit would be poured out upon all who believed in the Lord, all who "called upon the name of the Lord" (Acts 2:14-21). This is what has happened to the one hundred and twenty, says Peter. And on that day about three thousand others also believed in the Lord Jesus, and they too were filled with the Holy Spirit (Acts 2:38, 41).

Matthew and Mark tell us of the mission of the twelve apostles (Matt. 10; Mark 6). Only Luke tells us of the mission of the seventy other disciples (Luke 10). There is symbolic meaning in the twelve and in the seventy. Twelve is symbolic of Israel, descended from the twelve sons of Jacob. Seventy symbolizes all the nations of the earth, for the table of Noah's descendants in Genesis lists seventy nations (Gen. 10). Jesus chose twelve apostles to signify that the Church is the new Israel. But his Church has a mission to all the nations of the earth.

The seventy disciples sent by the Lord before his face are symbolic of all Christians, for all share in the Lord's own mission to all the nations. Therefore all are endowed with charismatic gifts of the Spirit for carrying out this mission. Vatican Council II taught that every Christian, by reason of his union with Christ through baptism and confirmation, is directly commissioned by the Lord Jesus to take part in the apostolic mission of the Church. Therefore each Christian has the right and the duty to engage in this mission, and has been endowed with the necessary charismatic gifts to fulfill the mission (*Decree on the Apostolate of the Laity*, 3).

When Moses expressed his desire that every one of God's people would be filled with the Spirit, it was under the pressure of his heavy burden of care for the great multitude of God's people. God lightened the burden by giving the seventy elders a share in his Spirit. When Joshua seemed to want to hoard the Spirit, Moses would not let the Spirit be hoarded. With Moses, we should desire that everyone will have a share in it.

Priests in our day often complain about the huge burden they must carry in caring for God's people. And it is true that practically every flock is larger than the priest can handle by himself. But God has provided the charismatic gifts and ministries of the laity to help bear this burden. Priests should not try to hoard the Spirit, but should learn to let God's people exercise their share in the Spirit. They should desire, like Moses, that all their people be prophets, or exercise other charismatic ministries. The people who have charismatic ministries need to cooperate with their priests and work in harmony with them.

Priests should not be like Joshua, jealous of their authority and power. They should not jealously try to keep everything under their own control, as if they were king in the kingdom of God. They should take to heart the Vatican Council's teaching that God has endowed all his people with charismatic ministries, which need to be discerned and coordinated by their pastors (*Dogmatic Constitution on the Church*, 30). The priest, presiding over God's people, is meant to be a coordinator of a multitude of ministries exercised by God's people.

"As Yahweh Lives and as You Live!"

Elisha ardently desired to share in Elijah's ministry, and followed him persistently, refusing to leave him, till at last Elijah gave him the opportunity to request a double portion of the prophet's spirit. Each time Elijah had tried to dismiss him, Elisha had said, "As Yahweh lives, and as you yourself live, I will not leave you" (2 Kings 2:2, 5,*j*). Elisha will not give up till he gets his request, he will not leave Elijah till he is promised the double portion. "As Yahweh lives, and as you yourself live, I will not leave you."

That is the way we should speak to Jesus, the New Elijah:

As the Father lives, and as you yourself live, I will not leave you, Jesus, till you give me the double portion of your

Spirit, till you clothe me in your mantle, and empower me to carry out my share in your mission. As the Father lives, and as you live by the Father (John 6:57), give me your Holy Spirit, so that I may live the same life which you and the Father live! And give me a fullness of your Holy Spirit, so that I may continue your own mission to bring all the nations into this life with the Father!

I will follow you, Lord Jesus, as you steadfastly set your face for Jerusalem on your journey to the Father by way of the cross. I will give you no peace, I will not leave you, till you clothe me with power from on high and fill me with your Spirit.

CHAPTER TWO

ELIJAH: YAHWEH'S SERVANT

"The Lord ... before Whom I Stand"

Now Elijah the Tishbite, of Tishbe in Gilead, said to Ahab, "As the Lord the God of Israel lives, before whom I stand, there shall be neither dew nor rain these years, except by my word" (1 Kings 17:1,*r*).

Every Christian is to go before the Lord in the Spirit and power of Jesus, the New Elijah. To learn what this means, we can meditate upon the various characteristics of Elijah, the prophet. The most fundamental of these characteristics becomes clear in the very first words Elijah speaks in the Bible: "Elijah said to Ahab, 'As the Lord the God of Israel lives, *before whom I stand* ...'" (1 Kings 17:1,*r*, emphasis added).

Elijah *stands before the Lord.* Thus he describes himself as the Lord's servant, ever standing at attention, ready for any service whatsoever that may be required of him. The Lord is the whole focus of his life.

Some versions have weakened Elijah's words, "before whom I stand," by translating them, "whom I serve" *(j,n).* This translation seems to put the emphasis on the service rendered rather than on the person served. "Before whom I stand" puts the emphasis on the Lord, and on attentiveness to him and to the word of his will.

A busy servant can only too easily put all the emphasis on the service he is rendering, and forget the Lord whom he is serving. Thus he becomes officious, serving where his services are neither asked nor needed, doing his own thing while claiming to be a good servant. He is busy about much serving, but is not really doing the Lord's work.

Or he can become like the servant described by Jesus, who sets himself up in the master's place in pride and officiousness, and begins to beat his fellow servants (Matt. 24:48).

Zealous servants of God can only too easily get so involved in service that they begin to set up this service as their god. Their own way of doing things becomes their god. They no longer listen to the Lord to hear whether or not this is what he wants them to do. They do not listen to the true needs of God's people, but engage only in their own preconceived ideas about what is good for the people and what needs to be done.

But Elijah stands ready before the Lord. He is not officious, not taking tasks upon himself which are not from the Lord. He stands ready only for God's word of command. He waits for his orders and goes only when he is sent. He undertakes only what God commissions him to do. Therefore it is only God's word and work that he undertakes and accomplishes.

Consequently, when he does go forth on a mission, he goes endowed with all the power of God's word and spirit. He can boldly say, "There shall be no dew or rain except at my word" (1 Kings 17:1,n). God's power is in Elijah's word, because it is God who has sent him; he has not taken his mission upon himself. He has waited upon the Lord's good pleasure, he has stood ready.

St. James tells us that this powerful word of Elijah is the word of prayer. "The fervent petition of a holy man is powerful indeed. Elijah was only a man like us, yet he prayed earnestly that it would not rain, and no rain fell on the land for three years and six months. When he prayed again, the sky burst forth with rain, and the land produced its crops" (James 5:16-18,n). Because he stands before the Lord in prayer, awaiting God's word, the power of God is in the prophet's word when he does speak.

Like Elijah, every true servant of God stands before the Lord waiting for his word of command. He comes in prayer before the Lord, consulting him before he does anything. He does nothing unless he is sure it is by the Lord's commission. And when he has accomplished a task for the Lord, he returns to the Lord's presence in prayer, ready for his next commission.

The Lord is the focus of his life, and his eyes are ever upon him: "Behold, as the eyes of servants are on the hands of their masters"—waiting for the slightest sign of the master's will—"as the eyes of a maid are on the hands of her mistress, so are our eyes on the Lord, our God" (Ps. 123:2,n). We do only what the Lord indicates. Otherwise we are not the Lord's servant, but are serving only our own ego, our vanity, our self-importance. We do not have the power of God's word behind us, nor are we moved by the Lord's Spirit.

"Yahweh Lives!"

Another aspect of Elijah's character stands out as we consider the nature of his mission as a prophet. This mission begins when he declares a drought upon the land of Israel. "Elijah said to Ahab, 'As the Lord God lives, before whom I stand, there shall be neither dew nor rain these years except by my word' " (1 Kings 17:1,r). It is very important that we look at this closely, for Elijah's fiery zeal has often been misunderstood. Even the apostles James and John were mistaken about his true character.

Elijah, it seems, was often looked upon as a vindictive prophet of destruction who called down fire from heaven to destroy his opponents. He executed the four hundred and fifty prophets of Baal after calling down fire to prove Yahweh's superiority to their god (1 Kings 18:38-40). And he called down fire to destroy the two groups of fifty soldiers sent to arrest him (2 Kings 1:10, 12).

In Luke's Gospel, James and John try to imitate Elijah. When a town in Samaria refuses to receive Jesus, they say to Jesus, "Lord, do you want us to bid fire come down from heaven and consume them?" (Luke 9:54,r). But Jesus turns and rebukes them. In some ancient manuscripts he says, "You do not know what manner of spirit you are of; for the Son of Man came not to destroy men's lives, but to save them" (Luke 9:54,*r*).

To understand the true spirit of Elijah, we shall focus our attention upon the true nature of his mission. His was a mission of life, not of death. Yahweh his God is the living God and the life-giving God. The first recorded words of Elijah are a reference to this *living* God. Elijah swears by the living God that his word will come true: "As the Lord, the God of Israel lives, in whose presence I stand, during these years there shall be no dew or rain except at my word" (1 Kings 17:1,*n*).

Elijah is carrying on a one-man holy war against the Baal worshipped by Jezebel, the Phoenician princess who has become queen of Israel. The Baal was a storm god, the god of rain, and therefore he was worshipped as a fertility god, a giver of life.

But Elijah's first weapon in the holy war is the word of God. By the word which God gives him to speak, Elijah stops all rain for three and a half years. He does this by the power of the God of Israel, the living God and giver of life. Because the living God has stopped all rain, it becomes manifest that Baal, the storm god, is powerless to give rain and life, and is indeed a no-god. The great famine which results spreads throughout Israel, and even to Phoenicia, the homeland of Jezebel (1 Kings 17:9, 14). Thus Yahweh shows that his life-giving power is not limited to the land of Israel.

Because Jezebel is putting to death all the prophets of Yahweh, Elijah must go into hiding. After staying for some time in the desert, he is sent by Yahweh into Phoenicia, to a widow living in the city of Zarephath, in the territory of Sidon (1 Kings 17:8-24). That other woman of Phoenicia, Jezebel, has provoked death in the land of Yahweh; now Elijah, prophet of the living God, goes to bring life into the land of the Phoenicians.

When Elijah reaches the widow of Sidon, she and her son are about to die because of the drought and famine. The prophet asks her for a cup of water, and she willingly goes to get this for him, even though water is scarce. He asks her also for a bit of bread. The earth has produced no crops, and the widow is down to her last measure of flour and oil. She is about to bake a last loaf of bread, "that we may eat it and die" (1 Kings 17:12,r).

But because she proves willing to share even that last loaf with the prophet, she is blessed by Yahweh with a supply of food that does not end until the famine is over. The living God preserves and nourishes her life, and her son's, and the prophet's. Jesus referred to her when he said, "He who receives a prophet because he is a prophet shall receive a prophet's reward . . . Whoever gives to one of these little ones even a cup of cold water because he is a disciple, truly, I say to you, he shall not lose his reward" (Matt. 10:41-42,r). Humble ministry, lowly service, is richly blessed.

The Phoenician widow is the antithesis of the Phoenician Jezebel. Whereas the queen is a murderess, and in her greed kills Naboath to steal his vineyard, the widow practices the great virtue of hospitality, the Old Testament virtue which is so close to full Christian love. She willingly shares the little she has.

She foreshadows that widow in the Gospel who put her last two mites into the temple treasury as an offering to God. Jesus contrasted that woman with the rich people and commended her: "Truly, I tell you, this poor widow has put in more than all of them; for they all contributed out of their abundance, but she out of her poverty put in all the living that she had" (Luke 21:3-4,r). The widow of Sidon, too, gave all the living that she had, to feed Elijah with her last measure of flour and oil.

Both widows exemplify absolute trust in the Lord of life. Bereft of human help, the widow is a symbol of human helplessness before God. But she not only trusts in God; she honors him by dedicating her tiny sustenance to his worship. In her very act of sharing the little she has, the widow of Sidon expresses her faith in the living God. "As the Lord your God lives," she says to Elijah, telling him how short her supply of food is (1 Kings 17:12). And when the prophet tells her that the flour and oil will not fail till Yahweh sends rain again, she

believes the word of the prophet, and expresses this faith by
feeding the prophet first, then herself and her son.

The Lord puts the widow's faith to a further test: her son
dies. In her grief she blames Elijah for the death. Through the
prayer of the prophet the boy is restored to life. The prophet
gives him back to his mother and says, "See, your son lives!"
(17:23,r). Truly, Elijah's God is the living God!

At her first meeting with the prophet, the widow had already said, "As Yahweh, your God, lives!" Her initial faith in
the living God has now been confirmed. "And the woman said
to Elijah, 'Now I know that you are a man of God, and that the
word of the Lord in your mouth is truth!" (17:24,r). The word
of the living God is effective even in this foreign land, the
home territory of Baal himself. Yahweh is the God of life
everywhere.

"He Gave Him Back to His Mother"

Jesus too raised a widow's son from death to life, and "gave
him back to his mother" (Luke 7:15,n; 1 Kings 17:23). The
widow's son lives, because Jesus is "the Living One" (Luke
24:5,n).

In telling us how Jesus raised up the dead son of the widow
of Naim, Luke is presenting Jesus as the New Elijah (Luke
7:11-17). When Jesus raises the widow's son, he "gave him
back to his mother" (Luke 7:15,n). When Elijah raised up the
son of the widow of Sidon, he "gave him to his mother" (1
Kings 17:23,n). At the miracle of Jesus, the crowds cry out, "A
great prophet has risen among us" (Luke 7:16,n).

The territory around the village of Naim where this miracle
took place was rich in the memory of two of the greatest of
Israel's prophets. Centuries before, at Sunem, a village about
two miles from Naim, Elisha had raised a woman's only son
from the dead (2 Kings 4:8-37). And directly down the Valley
of Jezreel from Naim was Mount Carmel, the chief scene of
the activity of the prophet Elijah. He also had raised a widow's
son from the dead, and, like Jesus, "gave him back to his

mother." Though over eight hundred years had rolled by since then, the memory of these two great prophets certainly was very much alive in those parts.

Therefore when Jesus gives life to the widow's son, the people cannot help but recall the prophets of the past. They cry out, "A great prophet has risen among us," and, "God has visited his people." Truly, God is in our midst, working in this man Jesus whom he has endowed with his own power!

They call Jesus a *great* prophet, not an ordinary one. He surpasses even Elijah and Elisha. With what ease and nonchalance he raises the dead! In contrast, how laboriously Elijah and Elisha had gone about the same task. Their first efforts to raise the dead met with no success. Only after long and repeated prayers and many prostrations and other ceremonies did the dead at last respond to their efforts (1 Kings 17:19-22; 2 Kings 4:33-35).

But it is different with Jesus. Raising the dead comes to him as naturally as breathing or speaking. With the simplicity of anyone else going through the most ordinary of actions, he brings the dead to life. "Weep not," he says to the widow. With a confident touch of the hand, he stops the litter. He speaks a mere word: "Young man, I bid you get up." And the man sits up and begins to speak.

The widow's words to Elijah of old could be addressed even more fittingly to Jesus: "Now indeed I know you are a man of God! The word of God comes truly from your mouth!" (1 Kings 17:24,n).

"No one arouses a sleeper in bed as easily as Christ awakens the dead in the tombs," says St. Augustine. "She is not dead, but sleeping," says Jesus of the dead daughter of Jairus (Luke 8:52, r). Then he says to her, "Get up, child." The breath of life returns to her and she gets up immediately (Luke 8:55). Of another dead person Jesus says, "Our beloved Lazarus has fallen asleep, but I am going there to wake him" (John 11:11, n). At the tomb of this man four days buried, he says, "Lazarus, come out!" The dead man comes out (John 11:43-44).

Jesus meant it when he said, "I solemnly assure you, an hour is coming, has indeed come, when the dead shall hear the voice of the Son of God, and those who have heeded it shall live" (John 5:25,*n*).

When Jesus raised the widow's son, "fear seized them all" (Luke 7:16). This was religious dread in the presence of the Lord of life and death. God alone is master of life. "You have dominion over life and death; you lead down to the gates of the nether world, and lead back" (Wisdom 16:13,*n*). "It is I who bring both death and life, I who inflict wounds and heal them, and from my hand there is no rescue" (Deut. 32:39,*n*).

At Naim, the people's dread in the presence of this divine power of life and death is filled with love and praise. For the Lord of life and death has indeed visited his people, not to take life, but to give it in loving kindness. He "was moved with pity" (Luke 7:13,*n*).

Thenceforth throughout his Gospel, Luke always refers to Jesus as Lord. He does not wait for the resurrection of Jesus to give him this title. Already in the Incarnation, the Lord God has visited his people. On the occasion of Mary's visit to Zechariah and Elizabeth, Zechariah celebrates this divine visitation: "Blessed be the Lord God of Israel! He has visited his people and redeemed them" (Luke 1:68,*g*). All this is the work of "the loving kindness of the heart of our God, who visits us like the dawn from on high" (Luke 1:78, *g*).

CHAPTER THREE

ELIJAH MOVED BY THE SPIRIT

Because he stood prayerfully before the Lord in total avail-ability, Elijah was able to speak words endowed with the fullness of God's power. And because he stood ever ready, waiting for the Lord's slightest wish, he was moved only by the Lord's Spirit. Indeed, he was famous for his amazing mobility in the Spirit of God. One never knew where the prophet would be next, for the Spirit would move him elsewhere in a flash. His reputation for mobility in the Spirit is manifest in two incidents.

Once, Elijah has been on the run for three years, hiding from King Ahab, who wishes to kill him (1 Kings 18:1). Every time Ahab thinks he has found the prophet's hiding place and sends to arrest him, Elijah has gone elsewhere. His mobility is astonishing.

Then the Lord tells Elijah to come out from hiding, and to present himself to Ahab. Elijah meets a servant of the king, Obadiah, and says to him, "Go tell your master, 'Elijah is here!' "

The servant protests that Ahab will kill him, because when he comes to find Elijah, the prophet will be gone again: "After I leave you, *the Spirit of the Lord will carry you to some place I do not know,* and when I go to inform Ahab, and he does not find you, he will kill me" (1 Kings 18:12,n, emphasis added).

When Elijah is taken up in the fiery chariot, his reputation for complete freedom in the Spirit is manifested again. After he has been caught up to heaven by the Spirit of God, the

23

brotherhood of prophets want to send out a search party to find him. They say to Elisha, "Let them go in search of your master. Perhaps the Spirit of the Lord has carried him away to some mountain or some valley" (2 Kings 2:16,n).

Elijah was completely free in the Spirit. Because he stood ever before the Lord in prayerful readiness, the Spirit could move him to any work in which God willed to use him. And at the end of his career, the Spirit caught him up to the fiery throne of Yahweh.

Yahweh's Fiery Chariot

Elijah's mobility in the Spirit is like Yahweh's own mobility. In Ezekiel's visions, Yahweh's fiery throne is a chariot, to signify God's complete freedom and mobility. In Daniel, too, Yahweh's throne has fiery wheels. "His throne was flames of fire, with wheels of burning fire" (Dan. 7:9,n).

Ezekiel emphasizes the mobility of Yahweh's chariot-throne. The earlier prophets and psalmists had used the symbolism of God riding on a cloud: "See, the Lord is riding on a swift cloud on his way to Egypt" (Isa. 19:1,n). Ezekiel too says, "As I looked, a storm wind came from the North, a huge cloud with flashing fire" (1:4,n). In the midst of it he sees the four cherubim (10:20), who are perfectly led by the Spirit, moved by him wherever he wills: "Each went straight forward; wherever the Spirit wished to go, there they went" (1:12,n). There are four wheels, one beside each of the four cherubim. "Wherever the Spirit wished to go, there the wheels went" (1:20,n).

The Merkabah (chariot) of Yahweh symbolizes a characteristic of God not symbolized by the Shekinah—the cloud of glory in which God manifested his presence among his people. The Shekinah symbolized God's immanence, his closeness to his people. His Name, that is, his presence, dwells in the temple (Deut. 12:11; Jer. 7:12). He comes down in the cloud of glory and dwells with his people (Exod. 40:34-38).

On the Merkabah of the cherubim, however, Yahweh remains free of all earthly bonds and soars above the highest heavens. The Merkabah symbolizes his transcendence and independence. Yahweh is subject to no man. He is totally free. Even though in astounding compassion and condescension he dwells among men, he must never be taken for granted. His presence is always pure gift.

He is not subject to man's whim, and he cannot be kept like a captive servant of men in the temple (Jer. 7:1-15). He is Lord, and not man's servant. In a vision, Ezekiel sees the Glory, the symbol of God's immanence and nearness to his people, leave the temple, and ride off in the Merkabah of the cherubim: "Then the glory of the Lord left the threshold of the temple and rested upon the cherubim. These lifted their wings and I saw them rise from the earth, the wheels rising along with them. ... and the glory of the God of Israel was above them ..." (Ezek. 10:18-23,n).

Elijah, like the cherubim of Yahweh's chariot, shares in the Spirit's total freedom. Wherever the Spirit wishes Elijah to go, there Elijah goes, moved by the Spirit. At last, he is taken up to God in God's own fiery chariot.

In Yahweh's holy war against Jezebel and the Baal, Elijah is worth more than all of Israel's chariots. As Elijah is taken up to heaven, Elisha cries out, "My father, my father! Israel's chariots and drivers!" (2 Kings 2:12,n). Elijah protected Israel and won spiritual battles for her, while her kings with their armaments were going down in defeat under the fiery judgment of God.

In moving Elijah about at will, the Spirit shows that Yahweh transcends all lands and places. He is not tied down to any shrine or any country. He leads Elijah even into enemy territory, the homeland of Baal, and there, through him, asserts his own life-giving power.

In the mystical life, too, God maintains his complete independence. We cannot use him in prayer as though he were our servant. We can appeal only to his love and mercy.

And we cannot enter into God's inner life just by using the techniques of awareness which are so popular nowadays. We can know God's inner life only when he freely reveals himself in the Spirit. He can be known only when he freely gives

97-916

himself. His presence cannot be forced by saying many words and by incantations such as those tried by the followers of Baal in their vain efforts to win the attention of their god (1 Kings 18:26-29). The gift of infused prayer, the experience of God's presence in our hearts, is pure gift each time it is given.

"Jesus, Full of the Spirit"

In sketching Jesus as the New Elijah, Luke brings out that Jesus, like Elijah, was always moved by the Holy Spirit, because Jesus too was completely available to the Father in prayerful readiness. He sought the Father in prayer before everything he did. "Jesus was *at prayer* after being baptized. The skies opened and the Holy Spirit descended upon him in visible form like a dove" (Luke 3:21-22,n, emphasis added).

"Jesus, full of the Holy Spirit, then returned from the Jordan, and was conducted by the Spirit into the desert for forty days" (Luke 4:1, n). The Lord's temptations in the desert are a foreshadowing of his whole mission of warfare against Satan. Moved by the Holy Spirit, Jesus goes into the desert to pray in preparation for this mission. He spends the forty days in the Spirit, in prayerful communion with the Father, before engaging in full combat with the devil. Luke points out that Christ's battle with the devil in the desert was only a preliminary skirmish: "When the devil had finished all the tempting, he left him, to await another opportunity" (Luke 4:13, n). The combat ends only on Calvary, where the defeat of Satan is definitive.

"Jesus returned in the power of the Spirit into Galilee" (Luke 4:14,n). "He came to Nazareth where he had been reared, and entering the synagogue on the sabbath as he was in the habit of doing, he stood up to do the reading. When the book of the prophet Isaiah was handed him, he unrolled the scroll and found the passage where it was written: 'The Spirit of the Lord is upon me ...' ... Then he began by saying to them, 'Today this Scripture passage is fulfilled in your hearing'" (Luke 4:16-21,n).

Luke shows Jesus at prayer repeatedly, before every turning point in his ministry. Before choosing the Twelve, "he went out to the mountain to pray, spending the whole night in communion with God" (Luke 6:12,n). "Jesus was praying in seclusion and his disciples were with him" when he called forth their profession of faith by asking, "Who do you say that I am?" (Luke 9:20,n). When he was about to set out for Jerusalem to face death, he "went up onto a mountain to pray. While he was praying" he was transfigured (Luke 9:28,n). "He rejoiced in the Holy Spirit," and praised and thanked the Father for revealing the mystery of the Father and the Son to the little ones (Luke 10:21,n).

Once he is taken up to the Father in glory, the prayerful Jesus is no longer simply led by the Spirit; he is now the Lord who gives the Spirit. "Exalted at God's right hand, he first received the promised Spirit from the Father, then poured this Spirit out on us" (Acts 2:33,n). The Spirit is now called "the Spirit of Christ" (Rom. 8:9), "the Spirit of the Son" (Gal. 4:6). "All who are led by the Spirit of God are sons of God" (Rom. 8:14,n).

In the Acts of the Apostles, Luke shows how the disciples, clothed with power from on high, are led by the Spirit in complete mobility like that of Elijah. The Spirit carries Philip as he did Elijah (Acts 8:39). The Spirit prevents Paul from going to certain places in Asia, because he intends to lead Paul to Europe (Acts 16:6-10).

We too will have this freedom in the Spirit, this complete mobility under his inspiration, if, like Jesus and Elijah, we stand before the Lord in prayerful availability. And when, led by the Spirit, we have accomplished our mission on earth, like Jesus and Elijah we will be taken up to the fiery throne of God and brought into the very life and presence of the Holy Trinity.

CHAPTER FOUR

ELIJAH'S WHOLEHEARTEDNESS

My God Is Yahweh!

And Elijah came near to all the people, and said, "How long will you go limping with two different opinions? If the Lord is God, follow him; but if Baal, then follow him." And the people did not answer him a word. Then Elijah said to the people, "I, even I only, am left a prophet of the Lord; but Baal's prophets are four hundred and fifty men. Let two bulls be given to us; and let them choose one bull for themselves, and cut it in pieces and lay it on the wood, but put no fire to it; and I will prepare the other bull and lay it on the wood, and put no fire to it. And you call on the name of your god and I will call on the name of the Lord; and the God who answers by fire, he is God." And all the people answered, "It is well spoken" (1 Kings 18:21-24,*r*).

In one of the great moments of his prophetic mission, Elijah assembles all the Israelites on Mount Carmel, and cries out: "How long will you straddle the issue?" Get off the fence! "If the Lord is God, follow him! If Baal, follow him!" (1 Kings 18:21,*n*).

All the people remain silent. Their hearts are divided between Baal and Yahweh. They want the best of two worlds, they want to have their cake and eat it too. They will not make a wholehearted decision.

Elijah, however, is no fencestraddler. He is wholehearted toward Yahweh his God. His very name is a cry of total dedication to the Lord. It means, "My God is Yahweh!"

Most Hebrew names were prayers and expressions of trust in God. Elisha means, "God is my salvation!" Isaiah means, "Yahweh is my salvation!" Jeremiah means, "Yahweh lifts up!"

But the name Elijah is not just a prayer and expression of trust. It is a *teruwah*, a battle cry. It is an expression of dedication to a holy war. It is a proclamation of faith and consecration: I belong to Yahweh! I am the wholehearted servant of his cause! *My God is Yahweh!*

Elijah's mission is to carry on a holy war against Baal, the god Jezebel has imported from Phoenicia. This was an era of syncretism. The cult of Yahweh and the cult of Baal had become more and more confused with each other. Even in the liturgy of Yahweh, the people were often really worshipping Baal, the fertility god of the Phoenicians. More and more elements of Baal worship were creeping into the daily life of the people.

Elijah cries out that two gods cannot live together peacefully. "If the Lord is God, follow him! If Baal, follow him!" Like Jesus in a later century, Elijah makes it clear that it has to be either/or. You cannot serve God and mammon (Matt. 16:24). You must make a clear decision. You must be wholehearted with your God!

A divided heart belongs less and less to the Lord. When we are not wholeheartedly committed to him, we tend to take the easy way out of every difficult situation, we follow the line of least resistance, we gradually fall away. We follow the god who will pamper our desires. Therefore in the holy war against Baal, Elijah's very name cries out wholeheartedly, "My God is Yahweh!"

Wholeheartedness is one of Elijah's basic characteristics. "I have been most zealous for the Lord, the God of hosts," he declares, when the Lord calls him to account on Mount Horeb (1 Kings 19:10,*n*). His name is the war cry, "My God is Yahweh!" I am his consecrated servant. "I stand before him" (1 Kings 17:1,*r*).

When God gives a person a name, that name signifies the person's mission and the divine endowments with which the Lord equips him for that mission. Thus Jesus changed Simon's name to Peter, Rock, and brought him to the unshakeable rock-like faith on which he built his church (Matt. 16:18). "Simon, I have prayed for you that your faith may not fail; and when you have turned again, strengthen your brethren" (Luke 22:32,r).

Elijah too had a God-given name which sums up the prophet's mission and personal characteristics. Elijah is wholehearted toward his God.

Wholeheartedness is a persistent biblical theme. "Walk in my presence and be wholehearted," says God the Almighty to Abraham (Gen. 17:1). The Hebrew word *tamim*, wholehearted, occurs again in Yahweh's prohibition of idolatry, magic, fortunetelling, and the like: "You shall be wholehearted in your service of the Lord your God" (Deut. 18:13).

The word *tamim* is often translated as "blameless" or "perfect." In itself the word means, "complete, full, without blemish, sound, whole." A human person, however, is complete and whole only when he is in right relationship with God, only when he is wholehearted in response to his Creator. Therefore the best way to translate this word when it is applied to a human person is "wholehearted." "Walk in my presence and be wholehearted" (Gen. 17:1).

Wholeheartedness is the most basic requirement of the covenant of God with Abraham and his descendants. This requirement sums up all the others. "You shall love the Lord our God with all your heart, and with all your soul, and with all your strength" (Deut. 6:5,n). There is no need to have a divided heart, for only One is God. "The Lord is God, the Lord alone!" (Deut. 6:4,n). Give him your whole heart!

Yahweh's Holy War

Wholeheartedness is Elijah's God-given grace for carrying on the holy war against idolatry and syncretism. This is God's personal war. He himself carries it out, and Elijah is only his servant. We see this in the story of Elijah's contest with the prophets of Baal (1 Kings 18:1-40). It is God who takes the initiative. He it is who sends Elijah to confront the king: "Go, present yourself to Ahab" (1 Kings 18:1,n). Yahweh then inspires Elijah to order Ahab to call Israel together: "Now summon all Israel to me on Mount Carmel," says Elijah (1 Kings 18:19,n). Through his prophet, God wills to confront his people and bring the issue of divided hearts to a decision.

Much as King Ahab fears and hates Elijah, he is impelled to listen to him, for he recognizes a divine summons in his orders. He experiences God's power in Elijah's word, and dares not resist. He calls all Israel together.

When all are assembled, Yahweh inspires Elijah to propose the question: How long will you straddle the issue? Which is the true God, Yahweh or Baal? When will you make your decisive choice?

And the Lord who proposes the question through his prophet is also the one who answers it. The people remain in silence when Elijah challenges them. Therefore the prophet proposes a test. The prophets of Baal will prepare a sacrifice for their god; Elijah will prepare a sacrifice for Yahweh. Then he who is truly God can show his power by sending fire from heaven to consume the offering.

The prophets of Baal accept the challenge, but even after hours of their prayers and incantations, Baal's sacrifice remains untouched. Then Elijah steps forward to prepare an offering to Yahweh. The very altar of Yahweh on Mount Carmel has fallen into ruin, so he rebuilds it and then sets the sacrifice on it. He even goes so far as to drench the whole altar with water, so that it is impossible to set it afire by any human means. Yet when he calls on Yahweh, fire falls from heaven to consume the sacrifice. The fire even laps the water still standing around the altar.

Since none of the people would witness for Yahweh, Yahweh has borne witness to himself. And he witnesses to himself as the living God, who not only lives, but gives life to others. For after sending the fire to consume the sacrifice, he sends the rains which he had withheld for three and a half years. Baal is neither the sender of storms nor is he the giver of life, which can survive only if there are rains. Yahweh has fed the widow and her son and the prophet for a year with that little bit of flour and oil, and he has raised the widow's son from death. Thus he has already witnessed to himself as the living and life-giving God.

Thus Yahweh himself carries on the holy war, and Elijah is simply his servant. Elijah testifies to this in his prayer for the fire from heaven: "Lord, God of Abraham, Isaac, and Israel, let it be known this day that you are God in Israel, and that I am your servant, and have done all these things by your command" (1 Kings 18:36,n). God has started the whole process, and he will finish it. It is he who always takes the initiative in his relationships with his people.

How different Yahweh is from the Baal of the Phoenicians! Yahweh is ever attentive to his people, always taking the first step in seeking them out and calling them back. But not so Baal! The prophets of Baal work themselves into a frenzy trying to attract the attention of their god. They hop and jump and cry out and chant their incantations and gash themselves with swords from morning till evening, but all in vain! Elijah taunts them about the shortcomings of their god. How limited he is! "Call louder, for he is a god and may be meditating, or may have retired, or may be on a journey. Perhaps he is asleep and must be awakened" (18:27,n). The words "he may have retired" are a euphemism for "he may be out easing nature." Elijah boldly ridicules Baal, for he has nothing to fear from a no-god.

Yahweh is not like the Baal who cannot be roused. Yahweh's people never have to go into a mad frenzy to attract his attention and to woo him. On the contrary, he is ever ready to manifest himself to his people. He is ever there, seeking his people. It is he who is looking for them, not they who are looking for him. He it is who has sent his prophet to set up this situation, in which he will show that he is the only one who is God in Israel.

Elijah's prayer continues: "Hear me, O Lord, hear me, that

this people may see that thou, O Lord, art God, and that Thou hast turned their hearts back again" (1 Kings 18:37,*m*). The people have fallen away, but rather than abandon them in return, Yahweh brings them back to himself. Lovingly jealous for his people, he is zealous for their good. He is ever faithful to his commitment to his covenant with them, even when they have been unfaithful to him. He is the living God, who always takes the initiative in his love-relationship with his people. In the presence of his people, he asserts himself on this occasion, inviting them to return to him.

Elijah's Intercession on Mount Carmel

In his prayer for the fire from heaven, Elijah says that he is doing all this only at Yahweh's command. He is asking for precisely what God intends to do in order to manifest himself in Israel: "Let it be known this day that you are God in Israel, and that I am your servant and have done all these things by your command" (1 Kings 18:36,*n*).

That is the way God always works in advancing his projects of salvation. He takes the initiative. By his Holy Spirit he inspires us to ask for what he intends to accomplish in us, though we do not always know clearly what we are asking for under his inspiration. "For we do not know how to pray as we ought, but the Spirit himself intercedes for us with sighs too deep for words. And he who searches the hearts of men knows what is the mind of the Spirit, because the Spirit intercedes for the saints according to the will of God" (Rom. 8:26-27,*r*). That is, the Holy Spirit inspires desires and petitions for what God wills to do in his people ("the saints"), even though what they desire and ask is beyond their understanding and power to express in words. But God knows what they are asking, for by his Spirit he has inspired them to ask. They themselves do not know clearly what they are asking, because what they ask is beyond human understanding. Yet they need to desire and ask for it, because desire opens their hearts to receive. By inspiring their desires and petitions, the Spirit opens their hearts to receive what God wills to accomplish in them.

Thus Elijah in his prayer can say, "I'm asking only what you commanded me to ask, I'm only doing what you told me to do." And he knows therefore that what he asks will most certainly be given.

Under what conditions can we pray like Elijah, in the full conviction that we are asking for what God has commanded? How can we be convinced that we are doing what God has commanded we should do to prepare the way for him to work in our hearts? How can we be sure that we are praying for what God's love intends to do in us, and in the hearts of the persons he has entrusted to our care?

We can pray in this way only if, like Elijah, we *stand before the Lord* in ever ready alertness to God's purposes, in ardent zeal for his glory. "I have been very zealous for the Lord!" (1 Kings 19:10,*n*). As wholehearted servants of the Lord, we need to seek his will alone, and carry out only that; and thus knowing what he wills to do through us, we can ask with full conviction and expectation that he will accomplish what we ask.

We can truly discern God's will for us, and for the people in our care, and what God wills to accomplish in our hearts, by listening to God in prayer, and by listening also to the hearts of our people, to their needs and their desires, consulting them and lovingly understanding them. The Christian leader who is truly attentive to the Lord's will, and discerns it devotedly, and strives to carry it out faithfully, will be able to pray for those in his care in full expectation that the Lord will do all that he asks. For the same Lord who shows us the work he commissions us to do, will inspire in our hearts ardent and expectant petition for the accomplishment of what he has commissioned. In prayer in union with Jesus, the Holy Spirit will inspire us to intercede for what God wills to give, and will thus open our hearts for God to accomplish in them the purposes of his love.

My God Is Jesus!

Elijah's name is his battle cry. Not just his name, but his whole life of service proclaims, "My God is Yahweh!" The

Christian battle cry is "My God is Jesus! Jesus is Lord!" With Thomas the Apostle we all cry out to the risen Jesus, "My Lord and my God!" (John 20:28). We are as wholehearted in our consecration to Jesus as Elijah was in his consecration to Yahweh, because Jesus is Yahweh, Jesus is Lord. Each of us can say, "As the Lord Jesus lives, before whom I stand!"

The correlative of "Lord" is "servant." "Lord" is a dynamic title. It signifies one who exercises power and authority. Jesus is Lord of my life, he has total dominion over it, I am completely available to his service. I share in his dominion and power, I possess his Spirit and power because I am his servant. I have crucified my own desires and ambitions, I have crucified my own ways of doing things, I am alive to God in Christ Jesus my Lord, I am wholehearted toward the Lord.

I stand ever in his presence, ready to do his bidding, going forth only when he sends me, doing only what he commissions me to do. And I am not distressed if sometimes he just lets me stand there. My heart is ready to be used, or not used, as he sees fit. I am consecrated only to his will. I do not undertake works of my own, on the pretense that they are the Lord's work. I seek out how the Lord wills to use me each day, for only when I am on the mission he gives me am I endowed with the Spirit and power of Jesus, the New Elijah.

When Elijah prayed for the fire from heaven to consume the sacrifice, he said, "Let it be known this day that *you are God in Israel*" (1 Kings 18:36,*n*, emphasis added). This is the same as saying, "Hallowed be your name!" That is our prayer to the Lord Jesus who is our God. Lord Jesus, let it be known in our day that *you are God in our world!* Carry on through us your holy war against the forces of evil in our day. You are the living God, the God who gives life. Carry on your war against the anti-life forces which, like Jezebel, are bringing nothing but death in our times. Assert yourself, Lord Jesus, so that you will be acknowledged as God and Lord of life. "Thy kingdom come!" Inspire in our hearts the desires and projects and the petitions which you will to implement in your holy war to win the world back to the Father.

By the power of his word in prayer to Yahweh, Elijah called

down fire from heaven, and the fire took possession of the offering which he had placed upon the altar. This was the sign showing that Yahweh is God in Israel. So too we place our hearts upon the altar before God, and the fire of the Holy Spirit, the fire of love, descends upon us, and takes possession of our hearts, enflaming them with love. This love is the sign to our world that Jesus is Lord, this love is the sign that he is God of all the earth.

This fire of love comes upon us because Jesus placed himself upon the altar of the cross, and the fire of the Holy Spirit was poured out upon him for all of us.

Only when God's own love has been poured out into our hearts in the gift of the Holy Spirit (Rom. 5:5) can we stand before the Lord in wholehearted availability to him for all that he wills to accomplish through us in his holy war. "My God is the Lord Jesus!"

CHAPTER FIVE

ELIJAH DISCOURAGED

"Only a Man Like Us!"

Ahab told Jezebel all that Elijah had done—that he had put all the prophets to the sword. Jezebel then sent a messenger to Elijah and said, "May the gods do thus and so to me if by this time tomorrow I have not done with your life what was done to each of them." Elijah was afraid and fled for his life, going to Beer-sheba of Judah. He left his servant there and went a day's journey into the desert, until he came to a broom tree and sat beneath it. He prayed for death: "This is enough, O Lord! Take my life, for I am no better than my fathers." (1 Kings 19:1-4,*n*).

By the power of his prayer, Elijah, the prophet of life, raised to life the dead son of the widow: "O Lord, my God, let the life breath return to the body of this child" (1 Kings 17:21,*n*). Giving the child back to his mother he said, "See, your son is alive!" (17:23,*n*).

And by the power of his prayer, he called down fire from heaven to consume the sacrifice he had prepared on Mount Carmel. Thereby he manifested the living and life-giving God: "Hear me, O Lord, hear me, that this people may see that thou, O Lord, art God, and that Thou has turned their hearts back again" (1 Kings 18:37,*m*).

By the power of his prayer he stopped the life-giving rain for three and a half years, and then by his prayer he brought rain again: "The fervent petition of a holy man is powerful indeed. Elijah was *only a man like us*, yet he prayed earnestly that it would not rain, and no rain fell on the land for three years and six months. When he prayed again, the sky burst forth with rain, and the land produced its crop" (James 5:16-18,*n*, emphasis added).

In spite of the power of his life-giving prayer, and in spite of the manifestations of the life-giving God in answer to his prayer, the time comes when Elijah becomes utterly discouraged, and wants to die. This occurs right after the defeat of the prophets of Baal on Mount Carmel. Elijah's victory has made Jezebel hate him all the more, and he must flee again to escape her. By this time, Elijah is ready to give up. "He prayed for death. 'This is enough, Lord! Take my life, for I am no better than my fathers!' " (1 Kings 19:4,*n*). His fathers, Abraham, Isaac, Jacob, the patriarchs, are all dead. Why should he expect anything better for himself?

Truly, Elijah is "only a man like us" (James 5:17,*n*). He feels the full weight of human weakness and discouragement. He has always been in hiding, a refugee, running from Ahab and Jezebel. Here he is fleeing again for his life. But is the life he is trying to save really worth the effort? He is ready to give up. He wants to die. He thinks his mission has been a failure.

But his God will not let him give up. This God, who always takes the initiative of love, sends his angel with bread and drink to strengthen him. In the strength of that food, Elijah then walks through the Sinai desert to Horeb, the mountain of God, where Moses received the covenant.

When he arrives on the mountain, the Lord says, "What are you doing here, Elijah?" (1 Kings 19:9,*r*).

This is a word of rebuke and a word of comfort. God's ways so often seem to be contradictory. He strengthens Elijah for the journey to the mountain, and then seems to rebuke him for being there! But that is true of all of us. After our initial responses to God's first invitations into his presence, he begins to make us more and more aware of the need for deep holiness if we are to live in his presence.

His words to Elijah, "What are you doing here?" are a rebuke, for the sanctuary of God's mountain is inviolable, and one does not enter God's presence uninvited. "When I summon [the prince of the people] he shall approach me; how else should one take the deadly risk of approaching me? says the Lord" (Jer. 30:21,n). "Moses himself was told, 'Come up to the Lord, you and Aaron, with Nadab, Abihu, and seventy of the elders of Israel. You shall all worship at some distance, but Moses alone is to come close to the Lord; the others shall not come too near, and the people shall not come up at all with Moses" (Exod. 24:1-2,n).

For no one could enter the presence of God without risking death. When Yahweh instituted the Day of Atonement, he said to Moses, "Tell your brother Aaron that he is not to come whenever he pleases into the sanctuary inside the veil, in front of the propitiatory on the ark; otherwise when I reveal myself in a cloud above the propitiatory he will die" (Lev. 16:2,n). The Lord goes on to say that the high priest may enter into the holy of holies only once a year, and only after offering a sacrifice of atonement outside the veil, bringing the blood of the offering with him as he enters inside the veil.

Moreover, according to the belief of the ancients, one cannot see God and live. "Moses hid his face, for he was afraid to look at God" (Exod. 3:6,n). Like Moses, Elijah covers his face for his interview with the Lord. "He wrapped his face in his mantle and went out and stood at the entrance of the cave" (1 Kings 19:13,r). Isaiah too, after his vision of God, fears that he will die, "for my eyes have seen the king, the Lord of hosts" (Isa. 6:5,r).

One cannot live in the presence of God's fiery holiness until he is more and more strengthened from within by an ever-increasing share in that holiness. " 'Who of us can live with the consuming fire? Who of us can live with the everlasting flames?' He who practices virtue and speaks honestly, who spurns what is gained by oppression, brushing his hands free of contact with a bribe, stopping his ears lest he hear of bloodshed, closing his eyes lest he look on evil—he shall dwell on the heights, his stronghold shall be the rocky fastness, his food and drink in steady supply" (Isa. 33:14-16,n)

But even the moral holiness, the rightness of living, here

described by Isaiah, is not enough. To see God, one needs an interior holiness at the very roots of one's being. One needs to be transformed by God's own holiness. Isaiah experienced this purifying presence of God's holiness, and expressed the experience under the symbolism of a fiery coal from the altar of sacrifice which purified his lips and his heart (Isa. 6:6-7).

Only in intimate communion with God can one be transformed by God's own holiness. Elijah is taken into an experience of this intimate communion: "Then the Lord said, 'Go outside and *stand before the Lord* on the mountain; *the Lord will be passing by*" (1 Kings 19:11,*n*, emphasis added).

"The Lord Will Be Passing By"

"Passing by" is a common Old Testament expression to signify a theophany, a manifestation of God's presence and power. On this same mountain, in this same cleft in the rock where Elijah is standing before the Lord, Moses had met the Lord four or five centuries earlier. Moved by God's lovingkindness, Moses had said, "Do let me see your glory!" (Exod. 33:18,*n*). "The Lord answered, 'I will make all my beauty pass before you. . . . Here is a place near me where you shall station yourself on the rock. When my glory passes I will set you in the hollow of the rock and will cover you with my hand until I have passed by. Then I will remove my hand, so that you may see my back; but my face is not to be seen'" (Exod. 33:19-23,*n*).

On a previous occasion, Moses had experienced another theophany on that same mountain, in which God manifested himself in fire and earthquake and storm. "Mount Sinai was all wrapped in smoke, for the Lord came down upon it in fire. The smoke rose from it as though from a furnace, and the whole mountain trembled violently. . . . While Moses was speaking and God answering him in thunder" (Exod. 19:18-19,*n*).

Elijah is told to stand on this same mountain where Moses had stood, for once again "the Lord will be passing by" (1 Kings 19:11,*n*):

A strong and heavy wind was rending the mountains and crushing rocks before the Lord—but the Lord was not in the wind. After the wind there was an earthquake—but the Lord was not in the earthquake. After the earthquake there was fire—but the Lord was not in the fire. After the fire there was a tiny whispering sound. When he heard this, Elijah hid his face in his cloak . . . (1 Kings 19:11-13,n).

When Moses was on this mountain, storm, earthquake and lightning had manifested God's presence. But when Elijah is on the mountain, these are only the heralds of the Lord's coming. They go before him, announcing his presence.

Perhaps because Baal was the storm god of the Phoenicians, and Yahweh was carrying on a holy war against Baal, Yahweh will not now manifest himself in a storm. He is rather a God who offers his people peaceful, quiet, restful communion with himself. There is no destructive fire to destroy Elijah who has dared to come up the holy mountain, but only a gentle, welcoming, comforting breeze.

The Sound of a Gentle Breeze

The "tiny whispering sound" (1 Kings 19:12,n) or "still small voice" (r) in which Elijah experiences the Lord's presence is "the sound of a gentle breeze" (j). We are told in Genesis that God used to converse on friendly terms with Adam and Eve "in the cool of the day" (Gen. 3:8,r), "the breezy time of day" (n). The breeze in which Elijah experiences God's presence symbolizes the intimacy in which God converses with his prophets, just as he had conversed with Adam and Eve.

The fiery God of Moses manifests himself to Elijah in comforting intimacy. If his words, "Elijah, what are you doing here?" seemed at first to be a rebuke, it was only to remind the prophet of God's inviolable holiness. Yet the words become a comforting welcome when the Lord takes him into the refreshing breeze of his presence, bringing him into deep communion with himself.

In this theophany, the Lord lets Elijah experience his transcendence. The Lord's power and presence infinitely transcend the fury of the storm and the power of the earthquake. God is an infinite ocean of calm and peace, and his communion with his friends is like a whispering breeze. In the intimacy of this calm, Elijah finds comfort and strength, and a renewal of spirit and courage. His despair disappears. He is filled with God's serenity and peace. He has a greater work still to accomplish for the Lord of Hosts. The Lord sends him forth again on the mission which he had abandoned in his utter discouragement.

Some sort of experience of God is at the source of every true vocation, and also at the source of every renewal of mission when we have given up in discouragement. We experience the transcendent God, we adore him in awe with covered face, we wholeheartedly surrender ourselves to him anew, we acknowledge his rights over our whole being; and he sends us forth again. We become fully and truly missionaries only at the moment when the Lord says to us, in the midst of our human failures and disappointments, our helplessness and discouragement, "Go anyway. I send you again. I am with you."

Then at last we go, not for human motives, not for the joy of action, not for the thrill of success, not for the praise of men, but sheerly because the Lord our God has sent us, for his purposes, and not for ours.

And we go in his power and Spirit, not our own. We have experienced our weakness and helplessness. We have experienced the bitter fruits of our stupidity in trying to do our own thing, in our own way, by our own power. We have tasted only frustration and failure. But when our pride has been brought sufficiently low, the Lord mercifully calls us again, and manifests himself anew. He sends us forth once more; and we trust now, not in self, but in him, whose power is perfected and manifested in our weakness.

Elijah, "only a man like us," discouraged and despairing, is sent forth again with "power made perfect in weakness" (2 Cor. 12:9,r). And once again he goes forth with a fiery power.

CHAPTER SIX

ELIJAH'S INTERCESSION ON MOUNT HOREB

"What Are You Doing Here, Elijah?"

What is the deeper meaning of this theophany to Elijah? And what does it tell us about Elijah's renewed mission which comes from it?

The account of the theophany in the text as we have it is framed between the twice-stated question, "What are you doing here, Elijah?" (1 Kings 19:9-10; 13-14,*r*). The theophany itself, therefore, should be interpreted in the light of this question and Elijah's answer. The theophany is God's response to Elijah's purpose in coming to see him.

"What are you doing here, Elijah?" asked God. Elijah replied, "I have been most zealous for the Lord, the God of hosts, but the Israelites have forsaken your covenant, torn down your altars, and put your prophets to the sword. I alone am left, and they seek to take my life" (19:10, 14,*n*).

Elijah had been sent by God on a mission to unfaithful Israel, who had abandoned the covenant with Yahweh and had gone after Baal. Elijah's task had been to bring about a renewal of the covenant and to restore the pure faith in Yahweh. Therefore when he thinks that his mission has been a complete failure, he comes on a pilgrimage to Horeb (Sinai), the holy mountain where the covenant had first been revealed to Moses. He wants to pour out his troubles to Yahweh at the place where Yahweh had already showed himself so plainly.

Strengthened by the food and drink given him by the angel, he comes to speak with God about the broken covenant.

St. Paul's reference to this incident is very enlightening as to what really took place: "Do you know what Scripture says about Elijah, how he pleaded with God against Israel?" (Rom. 11:2,n). It was like a court scene. Elijah was bringing charges against God's people. "He speaks with God to accuse Israel" (Rom. 11:2,b). He speaks this way out of zeal for the God of the covenant. "I have been most zealous for the Lord, the God of hosts, but the Israelites have forsaken your covenant" (1 Kings 19:10, 14,n). The prophet is saying, in short, "Yahweh, yours is a lost cause! And I am heartbroken about it. Are you willing or able to do anything about it?"

Instead of joining Elijah in his accusations against Israel, Yahweh takes his people's part. He reminds the prophet of his irrevocable election of his people. Though Israel is unbelieving, they are still God's chosen ones. Though the Lord is about to chastise his people with fire and sword, he will preserve a faithful remnant: "I will leave seven thousand in Israel, all the knees that have not bowed to Baal, and every mouth that has not kissed him" (1 Kings 19:18,r). This remnant will be a pledge of the future restoration of Israel. God's cause is not lost!

One needs to be very careful indeed in accusing God's people. "Who shall bring any charge against God's elect?" asks Paul (Rom. 8:33,r). Those who are so severely judging the Church today, and its leaders, will themselves be held accountable to God. "Who are you to pass judgment on another's servant? His master alone can judge whether he stands or falls. And stand he will, for the Lord is able to make him stand" (Rom. 14:4-5,n).

Yahweh's message to Elijah in the theophany is that he will make Israel stand. Even if the guilt of God's people is exactly as serious as Elijah claims, and they have indeed been unfaithful as a people, yet by his grace God will preserve a holy remnant for himself. His cause is not lost, his purpose will be accomplished. All this is his own doing: "I will leave seven thousand men in Israel," a faithful remnant.

The idea of a remnant had its origins in the barbarous wars of those ancient times.* Warfare aimed in principle at the total annihilation of the enemy as a people; even the youngest infants were killed. Often, however, the enemy was not utterly wiped out, and a remnant survived. Sometimes such a remnant became the nucleus of a people's rebirth. God will give Israel a rebirth through the remnant which he saves for himself. Even before he sends chastisement upon unfaithful Israel, he has determined to preserve this remnant for himself. The remnant doubtless consists of those who remain faithful, but their preservation in faithfulness has been decided by God before the start of the coming troubles. All this is God's own doing.

Just as Yahweh saved this remnant for himself in the days of Elijah, so too, says Paul, "in the present time there is a remnant chosen by the grace of God. But if the choice is by grace, it is not because of their works" (Rom. 11:5,n). God had not rejected his people Israel in Paul's time (Rom. 11:2), nor had he rejected his chosen people in the days of Elijah. The prophet had not been a failure, and God's cause was not hopelessly lost.

Fire and Sword

It has sometimes been said by commentators that the tiny whispering breeze experienced by Elijah was really a rebuke to him, correcting the fiery zeal with which he had called down fire from heaven to destroy God's opponents. But this is a mistaken interpretation.

The murmur of the tranquil breeze did symbolize the intimacy of God's communion with his prophet, but it did not indicate that the new action which God would take through his prophet would be gentle. The terrible orders which Yahweh gives to Elijah as he sends him forth again, show that Yahweh does not intend to be gentle with Israel:

---

*Von Rad, *Old Testament Theology* (New York: Harper & Row, 1965), Volume II, p. 21-22.

Go, take the road back to the desert near Damascus.
When you arrive, you shall anoint Hazael as king of Aram.
Then you shall anoint Jehu, son of Nimshi, as king of Israel,
and Elisha, son of Shaphat, as prophet to succeed you. If
anyone escapes the sword of Hazael, Jehu will kill him. If
he escapes the sword of Jehu, Elisha will kill him. Yet I will
leave seven thousand men in Israel—all those who have
not knelt to Baal or kissed him (1 Kings 19:15-18,*n*).

Only a purified remnant will escape Yahweh's chastising
sword. Earlier, all Israel had been given a chance to escape.
Elijah had gathered the Israelites together and had given
them the choice: "How long will you straddle the issue? If the
Lord is God, follow him; if Baal, follow him" (18:21,*n*). But the
people had remained silent. They had refused the Lord's
invitation. Even though the fire from heaven made them cry
out, "The Lord is God, the Lord is God!" (18:39,*n*), Elijah's
subsequent utter discouragement indicates that their conversion was not sincere.

Had the people accepted Elijah's challenge to follow
Yahweh rather than Baal, they would have found Yahweh in-
timately present with them as their covenant friend. But since
they remained silent and did not return to him, Yahweh manifested his fiery holiness by casting the flames from heaven
which consumed the holocaust prepared by Elijah. This fire
from heaven was a symbolic foretaste of the fire of judgment
upon Israel through the fire and sword of Hazael and Jehu,
and the fiery word of Elisha.

Yahweh is not finished with his people. Hazael, king of
Syria, is to chastise Israel from without; Jehu of Israel is to
chastise her from within (2 Kings 8:7-12; 2 Kings 9:1-10). But
this does not mean the end for Israel, since Yahweh intends to
"leave seven thousand men, all the knees that have not bowed
to Baal, and every mouth that has not kissed him."

Into our lives, too, God sends repeated invitations to turn
and commit our lives to him. To refuse these invitations is to
invite the disaster which is the fruit of human rejection of God.

Out of such disaster God's mercy and faithfulness will again bring a chosen remnant, chastened by suffering.

"Hear Me, O Lord!"

The faithful remnant announced to Elijah on the mountain will be God's own work, and no doubt we may presume that their faithfulness to Yahweh is the hidden fruit of Elijah's seemingly fruitless mission. It is also the fruit of his intercession. For in his prayer on Mount Carmel for the fire to consume the sacrifice, Elijah had asked God to turn Israel's heart back to him: "Hear me, O Lord, hear me, that this people may see that Thou, O Lord, art God and that Thou hast turned their hearts back again" (1 Kings 18:37,*m*). The prayer and the sacrifice had been commanded by God, and of course, therefore, they were accepted by him. In due time, Elijah's prayer and work did bear fruit in the conversion and the faithfulness of the seven thousand.

Elijah's intercession on Mount Carmel was supplemented by his intercession on Mount Horeb. For the prophet's complaint against Israel on the mountain of the theophany was indeed an intercession. Though the complaint is framed in the form of an accusation, it is implicitly an intercession for the restoration of the covenant. Though it sounds like a statement of hopelessness—"I alone am left"—the mere fact that the complaint is presented means that Elijah has not given up hope. He wants God to do something about it all. If he were still in total despair, he would not have taken the pains to make his long journey to the mountain to present the case before God.

The food given him by the angel had restored in him some measure of hope, just as the eucharistic food is the Christian's source of hope in the hardships of life's journey. Zeal for the honor of God impels Elijah's intercession: "I have been most zealous for the Lord, the God of hosts" (1 Kings 19:10,*n*). The prophet is pleading with God to vindicate his honor which Israel has desecrated by idolatry. God's personal glory is at stake.

Elijah's renewed mission is God's answer to Elijah's complaint. Out of the chastisement which Yahweh will inflict upon his people through the three men whom Elijah will anoint, God will preserve a purified remnant faithful to Yahweh. Elijah's intercession has been accepted. The prophet will not be alone! In a very real way, the faithfulness of the seven thousand who will not bend the knee to Baal will be the fruit of Elijah's work and intercession. His word, remembered in the time of tribulation, will bear its fruit.

Quite likely "seven thousand" is a symbolic number, signifying a great multitude. For seven is the symbol of perfection, and a thousand symbolizes an innumerable quantity. For example, when God says that he "continues his kindness for a thousand generations" (Exod. 34:7,n), he is not saying that his kindness to his people is limited, but that it is unlimited. "A thousand" symbolizes a huge number, more than you can imagine!

Courage in Our Mission

All of us are called to go before the Lord in the Spirit and power of the New Elijah, to bring about conversion of hearts in our times. In this twentieth century, we new Elijahs may well have to face up to the hard reality that in our day, too, God will preserve for himself only a remnant surviving the contemporary tribulations. We may have to face deep discouragement like that of Elijah, for the people remain silent and indifferent when we call upon them to make the decision for Jesus Christ, Yahweh our God. But the Lord will say to us, "Go anyway. Preach my word. Witness to my love. There will be a holy remnant. They will be the precious fruit of your ministry, and with them the new and eternal covenant in the Blood of Jesus will be renewed." They will be the hope of the world, the first fruits of the glorious renewal to come.

CHAPTER SEVEN

ELIJAH'S HEAVENLY INTERCESSION

"An Angel Appeared to Strengthen Him"

Then he went out and made his way, as was his custom, to the Mount of Olives; his disciples accompanied him. On reaching the place he said to them, "Pray that you may not be put to the test." He withdrew from them about a stone's throw, then went down on his knees and prayed in these words: "Father, if it is your will, take this cup from me; yet not my will but yours be done." An angel then appeared to him from heaven to strengthen him (Luke 22:39-43,*n*).

In a special way Luke's story of the agony in the garden presents Jesus as the New Elijah. Luke is the only evangelist to tell us that an angel from heaven appeared to Jesus in his agony to strengthen him. Is not this a conscious reference to the angel who appeared to Elijah when he was utterly dejected and wanted to die? By the food and drink he gave him, the angel strengthened the prophet to make the journey to the mountain of God. Jesus too is strengthened in prayer to make his journey to the mountain where he is crucified.

Luke wants us to meditate on the whole passion of Jesus against the background of the Elijah story. He wants us to *see* Jesus *taken up* in his passion, so that we may receive the mantle of the Lord's own spirit and power.

Earlier we pointed out that Luke's two references to Jesus

51

being "taken up" (9:51; 24:51) are an inclusion, the frame within which he presents the story of the Lord's passion and death. Therefore the words "taken up" manifest the meaning of his passion and death, for everything within an inclusion is to be interpreted in the light of the opening and closing statements. The journey *to* the cross and the journey *on* the cross are an integral part of his being "taken up." It is all one movement toward God: "Was it not necessary that the Christ should suffer these things and so enter into his glory?" (Luke 24:26,*r*).

If we wish to be clothed with the Lord's own Spirit and power, then, we need to see him not just in the glory of his ascension. We have to see him in his sufferings as "only a man like us," weighed down in the sorrow of his agony in the garden, and then making his journey to Calvary and to the Father.

"I Alone Am Left"

Let us therefore consider Jesus in his agony, and see how, like Elijah, he is "only a man like us" (James 5:17,*n*).

When Elijah is running for his life from Jezebel, he thinks that he is all alone, the only surviving servant of Yahweh. When he comes into the presence of Yahweh on Mount Horeb he complains, "I alone am left, and they seek to take my life" (1 Kings 19:10,*n*). Earlier, on Mount Carmel, he had already been keenly aware that he was alone when all Israel was gathered together with the prophets of Baal. "I am the only surviving prophet of the Lord, and there are four hundred and fifty prophets of Baal" (1 Kings 18:22,*n*). When it seems that his challenge to the people to follow Yahweh has been rejected, he feels more alone than ever.

Therefore he lies under the broom tree in deep discouragement. He wants to die. He thinks he has been a complete failure. He has had no success at all in his mission of covenant renewal.

Jesus too has been a failure. From the human point of view, his mission has had no success. His preaching has been rejected, and the leaders of the people have plotted to kill him, just as Jezebel had sworn to kill Elijah. His human heart can and does feel that he has failed totally. He feels terribly alone. As he suffers his agony, his disciples are all asleep, and give him no comfort and support. Worse still, he knows that they will all be scattered when the shepherd is struck (Matt. 26:31). "The hour is coming, indeed it has come, when you will be scattered, every man to his home, and will leave me alone" (John 16:32,r).

Jesus had to die alone. No man or woman could follow him in his death. He said to Peter, "I am going where you cannot follow me now; later on you shall come after me" (John 13:36,n). Only Jesus could go to the Father. Through his death on the cross he had to go alone, to prepare the way for us to follow later. "I am indeed going to prepare a place for you, and then I shall come back to take you with me, that where I am you also may be" (John 14:3,n). Only after his death and resurrection does he say at last to Peter: "Follow me!" (John 21:19).

Only the one who came from God has the power to return to God. "No one has gone up to heaven except the One who came down from there—the Son of Man who is in heaven" (John 3:13,n). The rest of us are powerless to lift ourselves from our created human nature into the life of God. Therefore Jesus dies alone and goes alone to the Father on the cross. From the Father he receives the Holy Spirit whom he pours out into our hearts so that we can be born again of God (John 3:3, 5). Once we are reborn in the power of the Holy Spirit as sons in the Son, only then can we go with Jesus and in Jesus to the Father. But this is possible only because he died alone, and went to the Father to prepare a place for us (John 14:1-5).

He had to die alone, not only because we cannot lift ourselves out of the human into the divine, but even more because we are sinners, excluded from the presence of God. We cannot go to God until Jesus has died as the victim for our sins, to bring us back into life with God.

"Sorrowful Even to Death"

Elijah is running from Jezebel in great fear, for she has sworn to kill him. Jesus too is overwhelmed with fear, for he knows he will be condemned to death.

Overcome with sorrow, Elijah prays for death, so that he might be released from the burden of his mission. Jesus too says, "My soul is very sorrowful, even to death" (Mark 14:34,r). Death would be a release from the burden of sin which he bears for us. He seems to be conscious of the weight of the sins of all mankind. The full force of all sin has been directed against him by the sin of those who have rejected him in hatred. The holiness of his heart, the purity of his soul, cannot bear the outrages which sin directs against the holiness of God. He is suffering all this outrage in his own human heart, for the more a heart is united with God in love, and the more deeply it experiences the holiness of God, the more it suffers from sin. Jesus, burdened down by this weight of sin, would find death a welcome release from the burden.

Unlike Elijah, however, Jesus does not actually ask to die. His words, "My soul is very sorrowful, even to death," are simply saying, "What a relief from this burden death would be! If only that cup of sin's bitterness could be removed so that I would not have to drink it!"

But he does not give up. He does not abandon his mission. He continues to pray, and in that prayer he is strengthened by the angel. In that strength, he goes like Elijah all the way to God's mountain. There, like Elijah interceding on the mountain, he intercedes for us even while he is being crucified, "Father, forgive them, for they know not what they do" (Luke 23:34,r). And like Elijah, he is taken up to glory, where "he always lives to make intercession" (Heb. 7:25,r).

"The Fervent Petition of a Holy Man"

Because Elijah was taken up to live always with God, the Jewish people came to believe that Elijah always lives to make intercession. This belief in the power of Elijah's prayer for God's people is manifest on Calvary when Jesus cries out with a loud voice, "Eli, Eli, lama sabachtani," that is, "My God, my God, why hast thou forsaken me?" Those standing by think that Jesus is crying out to Elijah for help. They say, "Wait, let us see whether Elijah will come to save him" (Matt. 27:49,r).

St. James, too, witnesses to this old belief in Elijah's power of intercession: "The fervent petition of a holy man is powerful indeed. Elijah was only a man like us, yet he prayed earnestly that it would not rain, and no rain fell on the land for three years and six months. When he prayed again, the sky burst forth with rain and the land produced its crop" (James 5:16-18,n). The intensity of Elijah's petition for rain seems to be indicated by his unusual crouched position, with his head between his knees (1 Kings 18:42). Perhaps Jesus prayed in this same position in the garden.

Both Malachi and Sirach depict Elijah as a mediator between God and his people: "You are destined, it is written, in time to come to put an end to wrath before the day of the Lord, to turn back the hearts of fathers toward their sons" (Sir. 48:10,n; see also Mal. 3:23-24).

We have repeatedly noted the power of Elijah's intercession during the days when he was on earth. By the power of prayer, he stops the rain, he raises the widow's son to life, he calls down the fire on Mount Carmel. He prays for rain, and it comes again. He intercedes on Mount Horeb and obtains the gift of faithfulness for the seven thousand.

We gather, too, that Elijah's intercession won the double portion of his spirit for Elisha. Elijah himself could not bestow the prophetic spirit upon his disciple; only God can bestow the Spirit. Therefore when Elisha asks for the double portion, Elijah says that he has asked a difficult thing. However, he implies that he will intercede with the Lord for Elisha in this matter, and gives him a sign by which he will know whether or not the intercession has been heard: "If you see me taken up from you, your wish will be granted" (2 Kings 2:10,n). When Elijah comes into the fiery presence of God, he presents the request; and Elisha sees him taken up.

Jesus, like Elijah, is taken up into glory, where "he always lives to make intercession" (Heb. 7:25,r), and asks for the Holy Spirit, to pour him out on us: "I will ask the Father, and he will give you another Paraclete, to be with you always, the Spirit of truth" (John 14:16,n).

Thinking that his mission had been a failure, Elijah had prayed for death; and then in the strength of the food given him by the angel, he had gone to Mount Horeb to intercede for the renewal of the covenant; and his prayer was heard. So too Jesus, weighed down with sorrow in the garden, is strengthened in prayer to journey to Mount Calvary. There he intercedes for the forgiveness of those who murder him. Continuing his journey to the Father, he now lives always on the mountain of eternity, interceding for the outpouring of all the blessings of the new and eternal covenant in his blood. He is the eternal High Priest who has entered into the holy of holies on our behalf.

"He Blessed Them"

St. Luke expresses all of this in one word. The Greek word "taken up" which he uses in Luke 24:51 has liturgical connotations, for this word was often used in the Greek Old Testament to indicate the offering or the burning of a sacrifice. Thus Luke presents the journey of Jesus on the cross as a sacrifice accepted by God.

Moreover, Jesus is shown performing a liturgical gesture while he is being taken up. "With hands upraised he blessed them. As he blessed, he left them and was taken up to heaven" (Luke 24:50-51,*n*). He is thus presented as the messianic High Priest, fulfilling and replacing the priesthood of the Old Law. For Luke's words evoke Sirach's description of the high priest Simon blessing the people in the liturgy of the Day of Atonement (Sir. 50).

> The greatest among his brethren, the glory of his people, was Simon the priest, son of Jochanan. . . . How splendid he was as he appeared from the tent, as he came from within the veil! (Sir. 50:1-5,*n*).

This refers to the veil separating the Holy of Holies from the outer tabernacle. Only the high priest went into the Holy of Holies, and that but once a year on the Day of Atonement, with the blood which he offered for himself and for the sins of the people (Heb. 9:7).

All the people of the land would shout for joy, praying to the Merciful One, as the high priest completed the services at the altar by presenting to God the sacrifice due; then coming down he would raise his hands over all the congregation of Israel. The blessing of the Lord would be on his lips, the Name of the Lord would be his glory (Sir. 50:19-20,n).

This was the only occasion in the whole year when the most Holy Name of Yahweh could be pronounced over the people as a form of blessing. No one else would ever dare to pronounce this Name.

The people would lie prostrate to receive from him the blessing of the Most High (Sir. 50:21,n).

Luke shows the disciples, too, prostrating themselves before Jesus as he bestows his blessing while he is taken up into heaven: "They fell down to do him reverence" (Luke 24:52,n). Because he is our sacrifice "taken up" by God, Jesus is our priest, pouring out the blessings won by this sacrifice. "Being therefore exalted at the right hand of God, and having received from the Father the promise of the Holy Spirit, he has poured out that which you see and hear" (Acts 2:33,r).

CHAPTER EIGHT

EUCHARISTIC INTERCESSION

All of us have times of discouragement like that of Elijah, we have times of sorrow like that of Jesus in the garden. We think we have failed completely. We are discouraged over our personal sins and weaknesses, or over the indifference of the people in our care. Our words seem to fall on deaf ears, and we see little fruit in our mission. At these times we go to the mountain of the new and eternal covenant, we go to Mount Calvary. We go to the Eucharist, which is the mountain of the Lord's sacrifice.

If the Lord says to us as he says to Elijah, "What are you doing here?" we reply like Elijah, "Lord, your covenant is being broken everywhere. Your words are rejected. The Jezebels of our time are spreading death right and left. Naboaths are being murdered and robbed of their vineyards, children are being murdered in the womb, sex is being perverted on all sides, no one is safe on the streets of our cities, children are abducted and sexually abused and murdered, husbands and wives hate each other and their marriages are ruined, children are beaten and abused by their parents. Nothing is sacred any more. Lord, all this desecration of human life is a desecration of you yourself. I have come to the mountain of the cross in zeal for your honor. I have come to intercede for your people."

When we come to the mountain of the Eucharistic Sacrifice, God's words to us, "What are you doing here?" are in no way a rebuke.

There had been a trace of rebuke when God addressed these words to Elijah. For no one could enter the presence of God without risking death. Only the high priest could enter God's presence in the Holy of Holies, and only after offering a sacrifice of atonement outside the veil, bringing the blood of the offering with him as he enters inside the veil.

Only Jesus, the Son of God, enters the heavenly sanctuary with impunity, and he comes into the divine Presence once and for all bringing his own blood in propitiation for our sins. Because of this, every Christian can now come into the divine Presence without fear. God once said that a person could enter his presence only when invited: "How else would one take the deadly risk of approaching me? says the Lord" (Jer. 30:21,n). But now all of us have been invited to come whenever we please. Because we have been baptized into Christ, our high priest, because we have been baptized in his sacrificial blood and made holy in him, we have free access to the Father in the Holy Spirit of Jesus (Eph. 2:12-22).

Priestly Intercession

Through the Sacrament of Holy Orders, the priests of the new covenant have been configured in a special way to Christ, the Priest and Intercessor. The character of Holy Orders, impressed into the very person of the priest, is the likeness of Christ precisely as Priest and Head of his people. This likeness is a sharing in Christ's own priestly power. Through the priestly action of the man in Orders, the priestly action of Jesus on the cross and in heaven is made present among us on earth. It is made active and effective among us. Thus in his priestly functions, the priest is a real presence of Christ the Priest.

Priests in a special way are called to be men of prayer and intercession, like Jesus and Elijah. They are not only free to enter the divine Presence on behalf of God's people, they have an obligation to go in, praying for their fellow sinners (Heb. 5:1-5). They have a responsibility to carry on the Lord's own living intercession on behalf of all of God's people. They are summoned into the divine Presence to intercede for their fellowmen. They should come before God on the mountain of the Eucharist burning with zeal for the holy war against the powers of evil. They should let Jesus, the eternal High Priest and Head of his people, express his own intercession through them for the people under their headship.

For the priest is like a living sacrament of Jesus Christ himself. The unseen presence of Jesus, the Head of his people, is made visible and effective in the person of the priest as representative of Jesus himself and leader of the people. The Lord's own intercession is expressed through that of the priest.

Christian Intercession

All Christians have a share in this priestly role. The baptismal character, impressed into the very person of the Christian, is a sharing in the priestly power of Jesus. It empowers the Christian, under the headship of the priest in Holy Orders, to join Christ in offering his sacrifice, and in giving expression to Christ's own heavenly intercession. In the Eucharistic Sacrifice especially, the priest represents Christ the Head, while the Christians who join him in offering the sacrifice are all members of that Head. As one with Christ the Head, represented by the priest, they go into the presence of God on the holy mountain, where they intercede for their fellowmen, and pray also for themselves.

Day after day many of us enter the sanctuary and join Christ the Priest in offering the Eucharistic Sacrifice to the Father, but we do it so thoughtlessly and coldly. Perhaps the Lord will say to us what he said to Elijah, "What are you doing here?" Will it be a rebuke because of our coldness and lack of zeal for his honor? Or will we be able to say with the burning love of Elijah and of Jesus, "I am most zealous for the Lord, the God of hosts. I am greatly pained because your people have forsaken your covenant, desecrated your altars, and put your servants to the sword"? For God's people are doing all that in our days.

We go to the mountain of the Eucharist in union with the
heartbroken Jesus in his agony. Nailed to the cross with him,
we pray with him for those who crucify him again in our days,
"Father, forgive them, for they know not what they do!" We let
Jesus express his own intercession through our intercession,
for we are living sacraments of his sacrifice. Our priestly action
as we participate in the Eucharist is a sacrament in which the
Lord's own priestly action is made present and fruitful here
and now in the needy world of today. Our intercession for our
fellowmen is efficacious precisely because it is the Lord's own
intercession which is expressed and made present in ours.

That is why when we pray, we always say (in the Church's
liturgy), "through Jesus Christ, your Son, our Lord." We are
living sacraments of the Lord's own intercession. Our prayer,
especially in the Eucharistic Sacrifice, makes present on earth
the eternal efficacious intercession of Jesus in heaven. It is our
responsibility to be burning with the Lord's own zeal for the
Father's glory when we come to the Eucharistic "mountain of
sacrifice."

In the liturgy before Vatican II, each hour of praise began
with the prayer, "O Lord, in union with that divine intention
with which you offered praise on earth to the Father, I offer
these hours to you." This was an explicit uniting of self with
Jesus in his prayer of praise and intercession. Whenever we
pray, it is good to begin by coming into the presence of Jesus
who is interceding, and then pray in the consciousness that we
are one with him, and he is praying in us and through us. Our
intercession is efficacious because the Lord's own intercession is expressed in it.

If, then, like Elijah, we are discouraged at what is happen-
ing in the world, the discouragement will fade away as we
enter the divine Presence bringing the blood of Christ. Summoned to the mountain by the Lord of hosts, with and in the
suffering and glorious Jesus, we go into the intimacy of the
Father, and there we experience his presence in that "sound
of a gentle breeze" (1 Kings 19:12). We are wonderfully re-
freshed and strengthened, and our sorrow and discouragement
disappears. We are then sent forth again on our mission like

new Elijahs, assured that seven thousand knees in our times will not bend to contemporary Baals.

In Elijah's day, the seven thousand faithful servants of Yahweh were in hiding, for fear of Jezebel. They were too frightened to witness for Yahweh. Only the fiery Elijah had the courage to declare himself. Not only his name, but his whole fiery person cried out, "My God is Yahweh!"

In our days too the Lord's servants are timid and in hiding, while the modern servants of Baal are bold and public in flaunting their immorality. Every Christian, consecrated in the priesthood of Christ, must declare himself like Elijah, "My God is the Lord Jesus! Jesus is Lord!" And the seven thousand who have not bent their knees to the immorality of our times will come out of hiding, inspired by our priestly Spirit and power.

There is no excuse for discouragement. Labors inspired by the fiery zeal of Jesus, the New Elijah, are never fruitless. "I have come to cast fire on the earth, and would that it were already kindled" (Luke 12:49,r). And since Jesus can pour out this fire of the Holy Spirit upon the earth only as the fruit of his sufferings and death, he adds at once, "I have a baptism to be baptized with, and how constrained I am until it is accomplished!" (Luke 12:50,r).

We can have the Spirit and power of the New Elijah only if we are baptized with the baptism he is baptized with. It is not enough to see the New Elijah taken up in glory. It is not enough to contemplate his resurrection and ascension. We must see him also in his weakness, as "only a man like us."

And it is not enough merely to *contemplate* him in his weakness and in his glory. We must *experience* his weakness and his power with him. We can be clothed in his power and Spirit only in the experience and acceptance of our weakness. When the Apostle Paul prayed to be freed of a weakness which was hampering his mission, the Lord answered him, "My grace is sufficient for you, for my power is made perfect in weakness" (2 Cor. 12:9,r). Therefore, says Paul, "I will all the more gladly boast of my weaknesses, that the power of Christ may rest upon me" (2 Cor. 12:10,r).

We must not give in to discouragement as Elijah did, we must not want to die to escape our burdens. With Christ we accept our weakness and helplessness. "For he was crucified in weakness, but lives by the power of God. For we are weak in him, but in dealing with you we shall live with him by the power of God" (2 Cor. 13:4,r).

We must not merely "watch and pray" with the Lord in his agony (Matt. 26:41), but in our weakness we must actually live his dying so that his power may be made perfect in us: "always carrying in the body the dying of Jesus, so that the life of Jesus may also be manifested in our bodies" (2 Cor. 4:10,r).

Only if we see the Lord when he is taken up, that is, only if we see his whole life, death and resurrection as one movement of ascension to the Father, and live all this with him in our own lives, will we be clothed with his own Spirit and power.

We notice that Luke frames his version of the Lord's agony in the garden between the Lord's twice-spoken words, "Pray, that you may not be put to the test" (Luke 22:40,n), "Pray that you may not be subjected to the trial" (22:46,n). This is an inclusion, and all that is framed between the twice-spoken words is to be interpreted in the light of those words. Between the Lord's twice-spoken exhortation to pray, Luke shows us the Lord himself praying as he is about to face the trial of sufferings and death. As is his custom throughout his Gospel, Luke wants us to get fully involved with the Lord, praying with him (Luke 22:40, 46), standing by him loyally in his temptations (Luke 22:28), following him steadfastly all along his sorrowful journey to his Father's house (Luke 9:23).

CHAPTER NINE

THE SPIRIT AND POWER OF ELIJAH

Then the king sent a captain with his company of fifty men after Elijah. The prophet was seated on a hilltop when he found him. "Man of God," he ordered, "the king commands you to come down." "If I am a man of God," Elijah answered the captain, "may fire come down from heaven and consume you and your fifty men." And fire came down from heaven and consumed him and his fifty men. Ahaziah sent another captain with his company of fifty men after Elijah. "Man of God," he called out to Elijah, "the king commands you to come down immediately." "If I am a man of God," Elijah answered him, "may fire come down from heaven and consume you and your fifty men." And divine fire came down from heaven, consuming him and his fifty men (2 Kings 1:9-12,n).

If we are to go before the Lord in the spirit and power of Jesus, the New Elijah, we have to know what his spirit and power is. The first incident in the journey of Jesus up to Jerusalem tells us what this spirit is not.

As the time approached when he was to be taken from this world, he firmly resolved to proceed toward Jerusalem, and sent messengers on ahead of him. These entered a Samaritan town to prepare for his passing through, but the Samaritans would not welcome him because he was on his way to

Jerusalem. When his disciples James and John saw this, they said, "Lord, would you have us call down fire from heaven to destroy them?" He turned toward them only to reprimand them (Luke 9:51-55,*n*).

Elijah is very much on the mind of James and John as they set out with Jesus on that journey to Jerusalem. Their imagination has been deeply stirred in seeing Elijah with Jesus on the mountain of the transfiguration (Luke 9:30). No doubt they are tingling with excitement in the conviction that this journey to Jerusalem is for the purpose of establishing the messianic kingdom in power. For the scribes, interpreting the prophet Malachi (3:1 and 4:5-6), taught that Elijah would go before the Lord to prepare his way, and would anoint the Messiah as King of Israel, just as he had anointed kings of old (1 Kings 19:15-16).

James and John are convinced, then, that Jesus is going to Jerusalem to be anointed King. They are so carried away in their enthusiasm that they themselves want to play the role of Elijah. They know the story of Elijah calling down fire to destroy the companies of soldiers who were sent to arrest him. Like Elijah, they want to destroy all opposition.

Only recently the people of Galilee have seen Jesus bring back from death the only son of the widow of Naim, in the very neighborhood where Elijah had raised the only son of a widow. And they have acclaimed Jesus, saying, "A great prophet has arisen among us!" (Luke 7:16,*r*). But now the people of this Samaritan town reject this prophet. Should they not be treated like those who tried to lay irreverent hands on the prophet Elijah? "Lord, do you want us to bid fire come down from heaven and consume them?" (Luke 9:54,*r*).

Elijah had called down the fire to show that he was truly a man of God. "If I am a man of God, let fire come down from heaven and consume you and your fifty" (2 Kings 1:10,*r*). Should not fire again be called down to show these Samaritans that Jesus is a man of God, the great prophet who has arisen among us?

But Jesus turns to reprimand them. "You do not know of

what spirit you are," he said (according to some ancient manuscripts of Luke 9:56). The spirit of the New Elijah is not to destroy, but to save.

"I Have Come to Cast Fire"

A little later along the road to Jerusalem, Jesus himself declares, "I came to cast fire upon the earth, and would that it were already kindled!" (Luke 12:49,r).

What? Has Jesus changed his mind? Will he destroy his adversaries with fire after all?

John the Baptist had used the Old Testament image of fire as a metaphor for the judgment which the Messiah would bring: "I baptize you with water; but he who is mightier than I is coming, the thong of whose sandals I am not worthy to untie; he will baptize you with the Holy Spirit and with fire. His winnowing fork is in his hand, to clear his threshing floor, and to gather the wheat into his granary, but the chaff he will burn with unquenchable fire" (Luke 3:16-17,r).

The words of Jesus, "I have come to cast fire upon the earth" (Luke 12:49,n) can be considered as they stand in themselves, and interpreted in a narrow way to mean only the fire of judgment which is to come. The words of Jesus would then be an urgent call to make a decision for him, and thus avoid the destroying fire.

However, in interpreting a gospel passage, we must always keep in mind the main themes of the evangelist and how he uses his materials, fitting them into the larger context of his themes. The broad, overall view of Luke's Gospel requires that we interpret this fire not as the destroying fire which burns the chaff, the sinners who refuse to receive Jesus. Jesus has already rejected this interpretation by rebuking James and John when they want to destroy the Samaritans with fire. Jesus never puts the emphasis on burning the chaff. He always emphasizes the gathering of the wheat into the granary.

Luke's is the Gospel of the Holy Spirit, and the fire which Jesus wills to cast upon the earth is the purifying fire of the Holy Spirit. Jesus will "baptize with the Holy Spirit," says

John the Baptist, and the Holy Spirit is a fire of love, not of destruction. He is a purifying flame which purifies hearts by filling them with love.

Jesus, we have seen, is always led by the Holy Spirit. In the power of the Holy Spirit he comes to Nazareth and reads a passage from Isaiah, "The Spirit of the Lord is upon me, because he has anointed me to preach good news to the poor. He has sent me to proclaim release to the captives and recovering of sight to the blind, to set at liberty those who are oppressed, to proclaim the acceptable year of the Lord" (Luke 4:18-19,r).

Jesus announces that this passage is being fulfilled in his person. In quoting from Isaiah, he deletes Isaiah's last line, which speaks of "the day of vengeance of our God" (Isa. 61:2,r). He stops at the words "to proclaim the year of the Lord's favor [the acceptable year of the Lord]" (Isa. 61:2,r). Thus he ends with the note of God's gracious mercy, and omits the reference to his wrath.

The Spirit and power of Jesus, the New Elijah, is the Holy Spirit of loving compassion and clemency. The Spirit impels Jesus in everything he does. We need to be possessed by this same Holy Spirit of love if we are to go before the Lord in the spirit and power of the New Elijah.

Even when the prophet Malachi says that God will send Elijah before the terrible day of judgment, he describes Elijah's mission not as one of destroying fire but as a mission of mercy, calling for the conversion of hearts, so that men can escape the punishment: "Behold I will send you Elijah the prophet before the great and terrible day of the Lord comes. And he will turn the hearts of fathers to their children and the hearts of children to their fathers, lest I come to smite the land with a curse" (Mal. 4:5-6,r). Elijah will prevent the curse, he will avert the destroying fire, by bringing about the conversion of hearts.

In Luke's Gospel, Jesus is the New Elijah who fulfills this mission of mercy, calling for conversion. When we go forth in the Spirit and power of Jesus, we are not enflamed with that false zeal that calls down fire to destroy the adversaries. We do not cast fire to burn up the chaff. Rather, we are wholly concerned about bringing in the harvest of grain before the fire of judgment burns up the chaff. We are to bring in the harvest before it is too late. Hearts purified and enflamed with love by the Holy Spirit will be wheat for the Lord's granary, but the unrepentant will be burned like chaff.

Therefore when Jesus sends the seventy disciples before his face to continue his own mission, he emphasizes the harvest. "The harvest is plentiful, but the laborers are few; pray therefore the Lord of the harvest to send out laborers into his harvest" (Luke 10:2,r). The mission is urgent, we are to waste no time along the way: "Salute no one on the road" (Luke 10:4,r). Jesus is like Elisha when he sent his servant on the urgent mission to the woman whose son had just died. Elisha had given the same instructions: "If you meet anyone, do not salute him" (2 Kings 4:29,r). The mission of the disciples of Jesus is also a matter of life and death: the eternal life of human beings is at stake. No time is to be wasted.

We do not know the day or the hour of the Lord's final coming to burn the chaff with unquenchable fire. It is not our business to waste time speculating about the day or the hour. Our business is to labor to bring in the harvest. The kingdom comes, not by our sitting on our hands waiting for the rapture, but by actively working to pour out the fire of divine love in the Holy Spirit.

The Spirit of Jesus

St. Luke records for us three precious sayings of Jesus which reveal to us the true spirit of his heart:

At that moment Jesus rejoiced in the Holy Spirit and said, "I offer you praise, O Father, Lord of heaven and earth, because what you have hidden from the learned and the clever you have revealed to the merest children. Yes, Father, you have graciously willed it so. Everything has been given over to me by my Father. No one knows the Son except the Father and no one knows the Father except the Son—and anyone to whom the Son wishes to reveal him" (Luke 10:21-22,*n*).

I have come to light a fire on the earth. How I wish the blaze were ignited! I have a baptism to receive. What anguish I feel till it is over! (Luke 12:49-50,*n*).

I have greatly desired to eat this Passover with you before I suffer. I tell you, I will not eat again until it is fulfilled in the kingdom of God (Luke 22:15-16,*n*).

The first of these passages shows what the fire of the Holy Spirit does in the heart of Jesus himself. The seventy disciples had just returned with great joy from their first experience of their mission. "At that moment," says Luke, "Jesus rejoiced in the Holy Spirit," and praised and thanked the Father for revealing to the little ones the secret which no one knows except the Father and the Son. The Holy Spirit, who causes Jesus to thrill with joy, is the Spirit of adoption, who makes us sons and daughters of God in Jesus the Son, burning with his own love for the Father and sharing in his own joy.

When therefore Jesus says later, "I came to cast fire on the earth; how I wish the blaze were ignited," he is expressing his ardent desire, inspired in his heart by the Holy Spirit, to bring the fire of filial love into every heart.

This fire is enkindled on his cross. And so in the next breath Jesus says, "I have a baptism to receive. What anguish I feel till it is over!" (Luke 12:50,*n*). These are precious words indeed, revealing the inner life of Jesus. Because of his ardent desire to pour out the fire of love for the Father, he fervently desires his baptism of blood and sufferings. He is aflame with love, he is stretched toward his passion with anguish, he faces his cross with steadfast courage, because he is so burning in his desire to enflame the world with the purifying love of the Holy Spirit.

Jesus will not destroy his opponents with fire from heaven. He has already determined in his heart to suffer their attacks with patience and courage. "When the days had come for him to be taken up, he steadfastly set his face to go to Jerusalem" (Luke 9:51,*c*). That is why he rebukes James and John when they want to destroy the opposition. On the mountain of transfiguration he had spoken with Moses and Elijah about "his passage which he was about to fulfill in Jerusalem" (Luke 9:31,*n*). He had gone up to the mountain, like Elijah on Mount Horeb, to pray for courage for his journey to Jerusalem. He was praying, says Luke, when he was transfigured (Luke 9:29). When he came down from the mountain, he said to his disciples, "Let these words sink into your ears; for the Son of Man is to be delivered into the hands of men" (Luke 9:44,*r*).

On his journey, he never draws back, but steadily advances along the way, "all the while making his way to Jerusalem" (Luke 13:22,*n*). The seventy disciples, that is, all of us, new Elijahs, must face the opposition in the way Jesus did, not with threats of a destroying fire, but with patient humble love which steadfastly advances toward the cross of persecution, not drawing back from doing good, in the face of overwhelming evil.

Jesus steadfastly goes on his mission to Jerusalem, even though his word will provoke opposition. He knows that he faces a baptism in blood at the hands of this opposition. He adds, "Do you think I have come to give peace on earth? No, I tell you, but rather division" (Luke 12:51,*r*). His mission of love provokes the violence of the evil ones. But Jesus does not run away to avoid violence. He must witness to the truth.

If the violent of this world are always to have their way because we run away in fear, then nothing of good will ever be accomplished. If good men are to be dissuaded from good because doing good provokes opposition and violence, then evil has triumphed for all time. If we do not battle courageously for what is good, then evil will be victorious.

There is to be no compromise in the holy war for our Lord's glory and justice! "He who is not with me," says Jesus in the course of that journey to Jerusalem, "is against me, and he who does not gather with me, scatters" (Luke 11:23,*r*). If we are not gathering in the harvest, then we are scattering it. There is no middle course. If we are not working very positively for good, then we are letting the forces of evil work freely.

The followers of Jesus, the New Elijah, will win the fire of the Holy Spirit for the world, if they share in the Lord's steadfast opposition to evil, and undergo with him his baptism of blood.

"To Eat This Passover"

The Lord's ardent desire to enflame the world in the Holy Spirit by the power of his baptism in blood makes him ardently desirous to eat the Passover meal with his disciples. "I have greatly desired to eat this Passover with you before I suffer. I tell you, I will not eat again until it is fulfilled in the kingdom of God" (Luke 22:15-16,n).

The Passover of the Jews will be fulfilled in his sufferings, for he is the true Paschal Lamb; and by his sacrifice, the kingdom is established. He ardently desires to be the Lamb. He desires therefore to eat the old Passover with his disciples for the last time, because he wills to fulfill it by giving himself as the sacrificed Lamb in the Eucharist, the new Passover meal. In giving his body and blood in instituting the Eucharist at the Last Supper, he expresses the meaning and purpose of his passion and death, which is to give us life and nourishment, and steadfast courage like his own.

The Passover sacrifice is fulfilled in the sacrifice of the cross, which establishes the kingdom. The eating of the passover sacrifice is fulfilled in an initial way by the eating of the Eucharist. It is fulfilled in a total and unveiled way at the end of time, when God himself is our food of life in heaven.

The Paschal mystery is fulfilled more and more as it is accomplished in each one of us. We are impelled by the fire of the Spirit which the Lord casts into our hearts from the cross and in the Eucharist. Enflamed with this love, we become new Elijahs, filled with the Lord's spirit and power. We burn with his own zeal to pour ourselves out in love on the cross, so that the Spirit of love may be poured out upon all the earth.

In the story of Elijah (1 Kings 18:38), fire from heaven manifested Yahweh as the true God, and Baal was shown to be no god. The flame of the Holy Spirit, consuming Jesus with the fire of love on the cross, manifests the Father as the true God, and Jesus as his true Son. That same love in our hearts continues this manifestation and witness.

CHAPTER TEN

JESUS AND ELISHA'S VOCATION

"When the days had come for him to be taken up, . . . Jesus steadfastly set his face to go to Jerusalem" (Luke 9:51,*c*). But the New Elijah does not make this journey alone. Great crowds were going along with him (Luke 14:25). Luke is insistent on this, because he wants his readers to join this crowd in following the Lord. He wants all of us to get involved in the Lord's life and journey.

Therefore at the beginning of his account of the journey, Luke incorporates three vocation stories. Everyone has a vocation to be a disciple and to follow the Lord. Luke wants all of us to answer this call and join Jesus in his journey.

In these vocation stories, Jesus lays down exacting conditions which must be fulfilled if we are to journey with him to the Father's house and share in his missionary journey as new Elijahs. The Lord is journeying to heaven, but there is also another theme in the journey story: Jesus is travelling through the world calling people together. This missionary journey will be extended to the ends of the earth only through his disciples, who are called to continue and complete the Lord's own mission.

Wherever they go in the missionary journey, they call people to follow the Lord in his journey home to the Father. They go before the Lord's face to prepare his way into the hearts of people. For the Lord can bring people home to his Father only if he dwells in their hearts through his Holy Spirit.

First Vocation Story: "Nowhere to Lay His Head"

As they were going along the road, a man said to him, "I will follow you wherever you go." And Jesus said to him, "Foxes have holes, and birds of the air have nests; but the Son of Man has nowhere to lay his head" (Luke 9:57-58,*r*).

"The Son of Man has nowhere to lay his head." One must be ready to give up home and all things to be the Lord's disciple. Jesus had no place on earth to lay his head, because his true home is his Father's house in heaven. "Did you not know that I had to be in my Father's house?" (Luke 2:49,*n*). Jesus said this at the end of an earlier journey to Jerusalem, the one he made with his parents when he was twelve years old. His parents thought that he was lost, and sought him for three days. When they found him in the temple, he said to them, "Why did you seek me? Did you not know that I had to be in my Father's house?"

This journey at the age of twelve is symbolic of his whole life's journey. His whole life on earth is a going home to his Father's house in heaven. He goes there to prepare a place for his disciples. "In my Father's house there are many rooms; if it were not so, would I have told you that I go to prepare a place for you?" (John 14:2,*r*). Like Jesus, his disciples have no place on earth to lay their heads, for the Father's house is their true home, too. That is why they leave all things to follow Jesus on his journey.

His journey with his parents at the age of twelve was a religious pilgrimage. They went up to Jerusalem to celebrate the Feast of Passover (Luke 2:41). So too the Lord's whole life is truly a religious pilgrimage, for he goes to Jerusalem where he himself will be the Lamb of God, the new Passover Sacrifice. At the end of the journey, at the Last Supper, he says: "I have greatly desired to eat this Passover with you before I suffer. I tell you, I will not eat it again until it is fulfilled in the kingdom of God" (Luke 22:15-16,*n*).

He himself brings about this fulfillment of the Passover by offering himself as the true Paschal Lamb, and giving himself to his disciples in the Eucharist so that they may eat of him, the new Passover Sacrifice. Those who eat the Christian Passover, the Eucharist, will be strengthened to leave home and all things and to follow him to his Father's house, just as Elijah was strengthened by the food given him by the angel, and walked forty days and forty nights to the mountain of God.

Elijah's journey, too, was a religious pilgrimage, for he was going up to the mountain where God had made the covenant with his people.

Religious pilgrimages were very important in the liturgy of Israel. Three times a year, God's people went up to Jerusalem to celebrate great feasts: Passover, Pentecost, and Tabernacles.

What do we do in liturgy? We celebrate the great works of salvation which God has accomplished for his people, so that we may enter into this salvation, that this salvation may be accomplished in each one of us. By the power of grace given to us in the liturgy, we are able to live what we celebrate in the liturgy.

Thus liturgical celebrations, and above all the Eucharistic celebration, not only express the meaning of our lives, but give us the power and Spirit to live this meaning. Or rather, the Lord present in these celebrations gives us his power and Spirit to live his life and to make his journey.

When the Lord Jesus was twelve years old, he joined in the liturgical pilgrimage of his people to the Passover celebration. In doing this together with his people, he gave expression to the meaning of the Jewish life he was living with them. But this liturgy in turn was a foreshadowing of the new Passover liturgy which he would establish by his journey up to Jerusalem to die as the new Paschal Lamb. His last journey to Jerusalem, when he went up to die, was not just a liturgy symbolizing the meaning of life. It was the full reality of his journey to the Father as the true Paschal Lamb. This is the reality which we now express and celebrate in the Eucharistic Sacrifice.

Thus the Lord's journey up to Jerusalem to die is an integral part of the Passover celebration at the end of the journey in which he offers himself as the true Paschal Lamb. That is why Luke includes between his two references to Jesus' being "taken up," not only his account of the Lord's actual sufferings and death, but his story of the whole journey up to Jerusalem in order to die. The notion of Jesus' life as a religious pilgrimage is very important. His whole life ending in his sacrificial death is his religious pilgrimage to the Father in which all of us must take part.

In liturgy, we said, we express the meaning of life. Jesus expressed the meaning of all human life, and the meaning of his own life as a member of our human race, by his religious pilgrimages—the ones he made during his life on earth as a pilgrim together with the Jewish people going up to Jerusalem for the festivals, and the one in which he went up to die as the true Paschal Lamb. All human life is a journey home to our Father in heaven. But this journey can be accomplished only in Jesus and in his sacrifice on the cross. We can accomplish the journey only in him, by the grace and power of his sacrifice. This power of his own journey to the Father is communicated to us chiefly in the Christian liturgy of the Eucharist, which replaces the old Jewish pilgrimages to Jerusalem. In the Eucharistic liturgy, we celebrate our journey home to the Father with Jesus, and in him we are given his Spirit and power to make the journey. Like Elijah, we "walk forty days and forty nights to the mountain of God" (1 Kings 19:8,n).

The journey which Elijah made from Beer-Sheba of Judah to the mountain of God, Horeb, is roughly three hundred miles, and can be walked in much less than forty days. Obviously the "forty days and forty nights" are symbolic. In the Scriptures, "forty" is usually symbolic of preparation for something new in our lives, like the forty days Moses fasted on Mount Sinai in preparation for receiving the covenant from God, the forty years spent by Israel in the desert being purified in preparation for entry into the Promised Land, the forty days Jesus spent in the desert in preparation for his preaching mission.

The rabbis, too, took forty days as symbolic of the time to be spent by their disciples in learning and repeating the instruction given by the rabbis.

No doubt Luke is giving this symbolic meaning to the Lord's forty days on earth between his resurrection and his being "taken up" in his ascension. During these forty days after his resurrection, Jesus instructed his disciples (Acts 1:1-8), opening their hearts to understand not only the Scriptures of the Old Law (Luke 24:45), but enlightening them also concerning the true meaning of what he himself had done and taught (Acts 1:1). He showed them that all that was written in Moses and the prophets and the psalms was fulfilled by what he himself did and said:

> Recall those words I spoke to you when I was still with you: everything written *about me* in the law of Moses and the prophets and the psalms had to be fulfilled. Then he opened their minds to the understanding of the Scriptures (Luke 24:44-45,*n*, emphasis added).

Luke would have all of us, the disciples of Jesus, spend "forty days" with him, learning from him in preparation for our mission, and in preparation for our being "taken up" with him into glory. Our whole life is a journey of "forty days and forty nights" to the "mountain of God," the Father's house; and during this period we are always under instruction by our Rabbi, the risen Lord, listening to his word and learning by walking in the footsteps of his own journey.

Second Vocation Story: "Let the Dead Bury Their Dead"

To another he said, "Come after me." The man replied, "Let me bury my father first." Jesus said to him, "Let the dead bury their dead; come away and proclaim the kingdom of God!" (Luke 9:59-60,*n*).

The man wishes to put off following Jesus until after his father's death. But the message of the kingdom is so urgent that its proclamation cannot wait. It is a message of new life which must not be delayed till people are dead.

"Let the dead bury their dead," says Jesus. This is one of

those riddles which the Jewish people loved, and which Jesus loved to use, for riddles were intended to challenge a person to profound thought. "Let the dead bury their dead" refers to something other than physical death. A mentality which was used to finding deep truth in riddles would realize that Jesus was speaking of the spiritually dead, those who had cut themselves off from life with God by their disobedience to his word.

Jesus' pilgrimage is a journey through physical death to life with God, but it is a journey to life because it is made in obedience to the Father. Those who follow him in his missionary journey are to proclaim this new life. "Leave the dead to bury their own dead, but as for you, go and proclaim the kingdom of God!" (Luke 9:60,r). Waste no time! Proclaim to the dead the message of new life! Physical death will lose its importance when it is swallowed up in the victory of the new life!

"Leave the dead to bury their own dead." The disciples of Jesus are not among the dead! On the morning of the resurrection, when the Lord's journey through death is completed, the angel at the tomb says to the women, "Why do you search for the Living One among the dead? He is not here!" (Luke 24:5-6,n).

"The Living One" is Luke's title for Jesus, just as "The Crucified One" is Mark's title for him (Mark 16:6). Luke and Mark bring out different facets of the full meaning of the Lord's death and resurrection.

The first Elijah, too, was a "living one." Elisha says to him repeatedly, "As the Lord lives, and *as you yourself live,* I will not leave you" (2 Kings 2:2,4,6,n, emphasis added). Elijah was a prophet of life. He carried on his holy war on behalf of the living God, the God who gives life. As his prophet, Elijah shares in this life, and is taken up to the living God. So too the disciples of Jesus, "the Living One," share in his life, and will be taken up with him into glory.

Elisha repeatedly refuses to leave Elijah. He swears three times by the living God, and by Elijah who lives, that he will continue to follow Elijah. He has hopes that he too will be taken up along with Elijah. So too the disciples of Jesus stead-fastly follow the Living One through death to life in his Father's house.

The angel at the tomb says, "Why do you search for the Living One among the dead? He is not here." Is this question a deliberate echo of the question Jesus asked at the age of twelve, "Why did you seek me? Did you not know that I must be in my Father's house?" A disciple is one who searches for the living Lord, and he finds him at home with his Father.

Neither the Lord nor his disciples are among the dead, and their mission as new Elijahs is to proclaim life. "Leave the dead to bury their own dead, but as for you, go and proclaim the kingdom of God!"

Third Vocation Story: "Let Me Take Leave of My People"

Another said, "I will follow you, Lord; but first let me say farewell to those at my home." Jesus said to him, "No one who puts his hand to the plow and looks back is fit for the kingdom of God" (Luke 9:61-62,r).

St. Matthew does not have this third vocation story. He presents only the first two. Only Luke tells this one, and he does so because it so clearly continues his theme of Jesus as the New Elijah. In this third story, the man who wishes to follow Jesus says, "Let me first bid farewell to those at home." This is what Elisha had said when Elijah called him to follow him.

So he went away and came upon Elisha, son of Shaphat, who was plowing with twelve teams ahead of him—he was with the twelfth. Elijah went over to him and threw his mantle upon him. Then he left the oxen and ran after Elijah saying, "Let me first kiss my father and my mother; then I will follow you." He replied, "Go back; what have I done to you?" When he returned, he took the team of oxen and sacrificed them, using the yokes of the oxen to boil their flesh, and gave to the people to eat. Afterwards he arose, followed Elijah, and became his servant (1 Kings 19:19-21,*m*).

After his encounter with God on Mount Horeb, Elijah departs from there and finds Elisha plowing. By throwing his mantle over Elisha's shoulders, he expresses Elisha's divine call to the prophetic mission. Elisha expresses his prompt response to the call by destroying the oxen and his plowing equipment as a sacrifice to God. This is an example of total obedience, and of detachment from his former manner of living, to devote himself wholeheartedly to the glory of God.

"Let me kiss my father and my mother, and then I will follow you." Elijah said to him, "Go back; what have I done to you?" This may simply mean, "I'm doing nothing to stop you." But the words seem to be more serious than that. Elijah seems to realize what a great yoke he has placed upon Elisha in calling him, and so in compassion he lets him first say farewell to his family before taking up that yoke.

Elisha turned and "took the team of oxen and sacrificed them." In many translations we are told that Elisha "slew" or "slaughtered" the oxen, but the Hebrew word really means "to kill as a sacrificial offering." He uses the wooden plowing equipment to cook the sacrificial meal, and invites his family to share in the meal. In giving the sacrifice as a farewell dinner to his family, no doubt Elisha was asking them to offer him willingly to the Lord's service, for in this sacrifice he was consecrating himself to the Lord. In sacrificing his livelihood, his oxen, to God, Elisha eloquently signifies that he has renounced everything to consecrate himself totally to the Lord.

After the meal "he arose and went after Elijah and ministered to him" (1 Kings 19:21,*r*). He serves the Lord by serving the Lord's servant. The nature of the service he renders to Elijah is indicated elsewhere: "Elisha, son of Shaphat, who poured water on the hands of Elijah, is here" (2 Kings 3:11,*n*). Elisha was Elijah's personal servant, waiting on his bodily needs. But he was also the prophet's disciple, in the full meaning of that word. A disciple shared fully in the life of his teacher, and thus learned not only words of truth, but the truth of life. He was formed in the master's own ways of living. He learned how to serve in humility and lowly submission, doing even menial tasks for the teacher, for humility is an essential element of openness to the prophetic word of God.

So too when Jesus chose the apostles, "he appointed twelve, to be with him, and to be sent out to preach" (Mark 3:14,*r*). They had to be *with him* to live his life and so learn from him. Their life shared with the Lord was the source of all their missionary power. Living the Lord's own life is essential in Christian discipleship. We have to be in daily communion with him in prayer if we are truly to share in his work of ministry to others. We are nourished by his own life as we eat his body and drink his blood in the Eucharistic sacrifice.

And we must be ready to minister to him in the most humble of ways, "pouring water over his hands" by humbly serving his servants. Willing service of others for the Lord's sake opens us to the Lord's word and Spirit.

Elisha literally left all things to follow the Lord as Elijah's servant and disciple. He sacrificed to the Lord his very means of livelihood. All of us must consecrate our means of livelihood to the Lord, not just our tools and equipment, but our very power to work, our skills and talents, our energy and technology, our body and its strength. All that we have, our utensils and our ability to use them, belong to the Lord, and are to be used only in his service.

Jesus seems to be even more exacting of his disciples than Elijah was of Elisha. Elijah had let his new disciple go home to kiss his family farewell. When we first read our Lord's response to the man who asked to go home and say goodby to his family, we get the impression that Jesus refuses him this permission. "Jesus answered him, 'Whoever puts his hand to the plow but keeps looking back is unfit for the reign of God' " (Luke 9:62,*n*).

Jesus seems to be saying, "You've put your hand to the Lord's plow to prepare the fields for his sowing of the word and his harvest of souls. Do not turn back from this task even for the sake of your family. Break all family ties!" In truth,

Jesus' succinct reply is a reference back to the story of Elisha's vocation. We must meditate on that story if we want to penetrate the full meaning of the words of Jesus.

Elisha does not break all family ties. He begins his mission by consecrating himself to his mission in the midst of his family, at a family sacrificial meal. His family joins in consecrating him to the mission, and will support him in it. The family is making a sacrifice, too; they are offering him to the Lord, they are giving up, for the Lord's sake, the help that Elisha would have given in caring for the family lands.

Every minister of the Lord needs to be supported by his family and his community in this way. Jesus sums up the whole Elisha incident in one sentence, zeroing in on the chief lesson from that incident: Once you have put your hand to the Lord's plow, do not look back to the material plow and the other possessions which you have left for the Lord's sake, or have given to the Lord. Look straight ahead to the Lord with steadfast purpose, plow straight furrows for the Lord. Jesus himself steadfastly set his face to go to Jerusalem. Follow him steadfastly. Be as loyal to Jesus as Elisha was to Elijah.

Once Elisha had said farewell to his family, he was forever after faithful to his vocation. He was so loyal and devoted to Elijah that Elijah could not get rid of him even in those last moments before he was taken up, when he so much longed to be alone preparing to meet God. Jesus had the same problem as Elijah. The crowds who needed him followed him so closely that they gave him no rest, no leisure for prayer. No wonder he had to spend his nights in prayer, for the people would give him no time to pray during the day. The Lord's ministers must find time to pray, even if they have to stay up at night to do it or rise very early in the morning.

Steadfast faithfulness is an absolute requirement in following Christ. "Whoever puts his hand to the plow, but keeps looking back, is unfit for the reign of God" (Luke 9:62,n). We need to be wholehearted in following the Lord, undistracted by other loves. All other loves must be consecrated to the Lord, and be directed by love of the Lord alone.

CHAPTER ELEVEN

ELIJAH'S MANTLE

"Elijah Cast His Mantle Upon Him"

Elijah set out, and came upon Elisha, son of Shaphat, as he was plowing with twelve yoke of oxen; he was following the twelfth. Elijah went over to him and threw his cloak over him (1 Kings 19:19,*n*).

Elijah was "wearing a hairy garment, with a leather girdle about his loins" (2 Kings 1:8,*n*). This, it seems, was traditional dress for the prophets. John the Baptist dressed in the same way (Matt. 3:4). Zechariah tells how false prophets, once they have been converted from their false ways, will no longer "put on a hairy mantle in order to deceive" (Zech. 13:4,*r*).

Evidently the hairy mantle was part of a prophet's official dress. Therefore to cast the hairy mantle upon another would be an investiture and an initiation into the brotherhood of prophets. But first of all it would indicate a divine call, for the prophetic function and spirit comes only from God. Thus, Elijah's act of throwing his mantle over Elisha indicated Elisha's divine call to share in the prophetic mission. God himself was taking possession of Elisha in his symbolic act.

An investiture is the act of clothing a person in ceremonial garments as a sign that he is being established in some office. The bishop clothes a newly ordained priest in vestments, the head of a university clothes a graduate in cap and gown, a monk or nun is clothed in a habit, a bride in white dress and veil. Universal customs like this show that there can be powerful symbolism in clothing. Investiture can signify that one receives authority and power to exercise an office. Elisha takes up the mantle of Elijah as a sign that he has received Elijah's spirit and power (2 Kings 2:13-14).

John the Baptist is described as dressing exactly like Elijah. "John was clothed in a garment of camel's hair, and wore a leather belt around his waist" (Matt. 3:4,n; compare 2 Kings 1:8). Referring to John the Baptist, Jesus said, "What did you go out into the wilderness to behold? . . . To see a man clothed in soft raiment? Behold, those who wear soft raiment are in kings' houses. Why then did you go out? To see a prophet? Yes, I tell you, and more than a prophet" (Matt. 11:7-9,r).

Clothing is not only symbolic in expressing what is in the heart. It can actually influence the heart and the way we act. Those who wear soft and luxurious garments are more easily inclined to self-indulgence than those who dress austerely. The hairy garment of the prophet was a sign and means of withdrawal from luxury and self-indulgence in order to be open to God and his Spirit. When Jesus said, "Those who wear soft garments are in Kings' houses," he was probably thinking about Herod. Herod, in his soft garments and luxurious palaces, fell into adultery with his brother's wife (Mark 6:18), while John, in his austere life in the desert, received the word of the Lord and the courage to confront Herod with his sin. Withdrawal from ease and comfort brings openness to the Lord and his inspirations.

There is a time and place for soft garments, of course. A wife, for example, could be expressing true virtue in dressing in a slinky nightgown as part of her way of expressing her sexual attraction to her husband. Sexual union between husband and wife, and the love it expresses, are God-given and holy. The proper dress in preparation for this holy union is not sackcloth or some kind of armor, which say, "Stay away from me," but a sensual garment which says, "I love you and am open to you."

The same wife on another occasion might dress in sackcloth for prayer and fasting, in order to be open for the Lord's inspirations. Paul writes to Christian spouses, "Do not deprive one another [of sexual union], unless perhaps by mutual consent for a time, to devote yourselves to prayer" (1 Cor. 7:5,*n*).

Since clothing is a very personal item, it serves to symbolize one's very self. When Jonathan made his covenant with David, he gave him his mantle as a sign that he was sharing his very self with him in a bond of close friendship (1 Sam. 18:4). When the followers of Jehu spread their garments under his feet and cried out, "Jehu is king!" (2 Kings 9:13), they symbolized the submission of their persons to his authority. The disciples expressed the same meaning when "they spread their garments on the road" before Jesus and acclaimed him King: "Blessed is the King who comes in the name of the Lord" (Luke 19:36-38). Thus they signified their readiness to lay down their very lives in his service.

"I Spread My Cloak Over You"

Since garments symbolize one's very self, when Elijah casts his mantle over Elisha, it is like clothing him in his own personality. More than that, it signifies that he is taking possession of Elisha and assuming responsibility for him. This same symbolism is manifested when Ruth says to Boaz, "Spread the corner of your cloak over me, for you are my next of kin" (Ruth 3:9). She is really saying, "Be my protector by marrying me according to the duty of a near kinsman. She is telling him that he is her *go'el*, and therefore he should fulfill his responsibilities toward her.

She calls him her "next of kin." The Hebrew word for this is *go'el*, which also means "redeemer" (Isa. 41:14; Job 19:25; Ps. 19:14). The Hebrew word *go'el* always includes two ideas: a close bond, usually of blood, and an obligation to come to the other's assistance. *Go'el* means the next of kin whose obligation it was to rescue from poverty, to redeem from slavery, or to avenge a death. Under certain circumstances, the *go'el* also had to marry his brother's wife when the brother died without heirs (Lev. 25:25).

When God enters his covenant with Israel, he becomes her blood relative, her next of kin, and therefore her *go'el*, responsible for her redemption from captivity, from sin, from shame. For by the covenant, God has set up a family bond with his people, and has bound himself to be their father and redeemer: "You, Lord, are our father; our redeemer you are named forever" (Isa. 63:16,*n*; see also 60:16).

The word *go'el* is applied to God about a dozen times by Deutero-Isaiah, speaking to Israel in her Babylonian captivity. By reason of his covenant-family bond with her, the Lord has the responsibility to redeem her, and he proclaims that he will fulfill this responsibility. "Fear not, O worm Jacob, O maggot Israel; I will help you, says the Lord; your redeemer is the Holy One of Israel" (Isa. 41:14,*n*).

Just as Boaz spread the corner of his cloak over Ruth, taking her under his protection by marrying her as her *go'el*, so Yahweh says to Israel, "I spread the corner of my cloak over you to cover your nakedness" (Ezek. 16:8,*n*). Thus he signifies his intention of marriage and of taking her forever under his protection as his next of kin, "bone of my bones, flesh of my flesh" (Gen. 2:23,*r*). "I swore an oath to you and entered into a covenant with you, and you became mine, says the Lord" (Ezek. 16:8,*n*).

So too Elijah, spreading his cloak over Elisha, is assuming responsibility for him and acquiring rights over him. Henceforth Elisha is his servant in the Lord's service.

"Clothed with Power from on High"

Against this Old Testament background of the symbolism of clothing, we can find rich meaning in the words of Jesus when he tells his disciples, "Remain here in the city until you are clothed with power from on high" (Luke 24:49,*n*). When they see him "taken up," it is the sign that they will wear his mantle, they will continue his mission, they will be invested with his Spirit and power, they will have authority to fulfill his work, he will take possession of them as his own, he will assume responsibility for them and will be their *go'el*.

Adam and Eve were ashamed of their nakedness, for by their sin they had stripped themselves of glory. When Yahweh found Israel in this nakedness and abandonment, he had covered her, taking her under his cloak with himself. He had robed her in his own splendor: "You were renowned among the nations for your beauty, perfect as it was, because of my splendor which I had bestowed on you, says the Lord" (Ezek. 16:14,n).

Jesus himself in his resurrection can be described in the words of the psalm, "You are clothed with majesty and glory, robed in light as with a cloak" (Ps. 104:1,n). In the transfiguration, "his clothes became dazzling white" (Mark 9:3,n). So too his bride the Church is clothed in his glory. She is the "woman clothed with the sun" (Rev. 12:1). Once the Bridegroom was "only a man like us," sharing in all our weakness. Now that he is clothed in splendor he casts his mantle of power over his bride, the Church. In clothing her with the Holy Spirit, he takes possession of her as his bride. He is her *go'el*, her protector, and assumes total responsibility for her. She has nothing to fear.

If the Lord clothes us with his Spirit and power and assumes responsibility for us as his disciples and bride, we in turn have responsibilities toward him, for he has rights over us. Elijah signified his rights over Elisha by casting his mantle upon him, and Elisha responded by following him faithfully as his servant. So we follow the Divine Bridegroom in steadfast faithfulness.

If clothing signifies a person's very self, to "put on the Lord Jesus Christ" is to put on his life, his personality, his virtues, his love. It is to live in him, and he in us.

CHAPTER TWELVE

JESUS AND THE HOLY WAR

In sacrificing his oxen to God and burning his plowing equipment, Elisha is dedicating himself to the holy war which Elijah is waging. This is a war against the idolatry into which Jezebel had led the people of Israel. In the early days of Israel, when God's people were waging the holy wars in conquest of the promised land, they gave Yahweh a warlike title, "Lord of Armies." Centuries later on Mount Horeb, Elijah speaks of God with this ancient title: "I have been zealous for the Lord, the God of hosts" (1 Kings 19:10,n). The Lord, responding to Elijah, uses warlike terms when he tells him to anoint Elisha as prophet to succeed him: "Him who escapes the sword of Jehu shall Elisha slay" (1 Kings 19:17,r). Elisha shall slay by the power of God's word, which is like a two-edged sword: "I smote them through the prophets, I slew them by the words of my mouth" (Hosea 6:5,n).

Elisha sacrifices his oxen as a sign that he is a true soldier in the holy war, wholeheartedly dedicated to Yahweh, unimpeded by a divided heart. By the sacrifice of his means of livelihood, he is totally freed for the Lord's service. This is clear from a consideration of the qualifications laid down in the law of Moses for soldiers in the Holy War:

> . . . the officials shall say to the soldiers, "Is there anyone who has built a new house and not yet had the housewarming? Let him return home, lest he die in battle and another dedicate it. Is there anyone who has planted a vineyard and

never yet enjoyed its fruits? Let him return home, lest he die in battle and another enjoy its fruits in his stead. Is there anyone who has betrothed a woman and not yet taken her as his wife? Let him return home lest he die in battle and another take her to wife." In fine, the officials shall say to the soldiers, "Is there anyone who is afraid and weak-hearted? Let him return home, lest he make his fellows as fainthearted as himself" (Deut. 20:2-8,*n*).

A man of divided heart will not make a good soldier. If a man is overly concerned about his house, his fields, his wife, his heart will be divided, and he will be unfit for battle. These stipulations pointing out who is free to engage in the holy war are really very wise and humane provisions for the welfare of the whole people. Houses and lands and vineyards need to be well-established, and marriages need to be very carefully nurtured and strengthened, before one turns his attention to other matters. For the good of the whole country, a man should be alone with his bride, and fully free to strengthen his union and love for her, before he leaves her for any length of time for public service:

When a man is newly wed, he need not go out on a military expedition, nor shall any public duty be imposed on him. He shall be exempt for one year for the sake of his family, to bring joy to the wife he has married (Deut. 24:5,*n*).

Likewise, newly planted vines and newly established homes need to be well-settled before the man responsible for them is free to devote himself to other things. The welfare of the whole people depends upon this. For the stability of the nation, a man must first fulfill his family responsibilities, strengthening his family bonds and putting his property and equipment in order, before he engages in public service.

In most cultures, unfortunately, it is the youngest who are required to go to war, not the mature and well-established. Many a wartime marriage has been destroyed by the husband's absence in military service because the young couple was not free to nuture their marriage in its early stages.

Strong families and well-established homes are the solid foundation of the whole society. All these things, family and land and houses, are consecrated to the Lord, they are his, they are a sacrificial offering to God. They are best used in God's service when they are well-cared for, for the good of the whole people.

Since this concern for a strong foundation for human life is God's own concern, we can see why certain people are not called to leave all things to follow the Lord as missionaries, but are sent home by the Lord to care for the family and lands and homes that God has entrusted to them.

On the other hand, we can see too how in every century God has called many persons literally to leave all things as Elisha did, and dedicate themselves totally to his holy war, stripping themselves of all things by the commitment to priestly celibacy, or by the religious vows of poverty, celibacy and obedience.

Every Christian is called to be a disciple of the Lord, not just those who follow him in celibacy and poverty and vowed obedience. And so the spirit of detachment expressed by Elisha in offering his oxen in sacrifice is necessary for every Christian. When all that God has given us, family, lands and homes, are truly consecrated to the Lord as his own, they are well cared for precisely so that they can be of the greatest service to the Lord and his people.

"I Have Married A Wife"

To those who have stood loyally with him in his temptations, says Jesus, he will grant the privilege of eating and drinking the eternal banquet with him in his kingdom (Luke 22:28-30). To accept the invitation to this heavenly meal, one must burn his plow and sacrifice his oxen, like Elisha. He must not be like the people in the parable of the invitation to the banquet (Luke 14:16-24), who say, "I have bought some land . . . . I have brought five yoke of oxen . . . . I am newly married and so cannot come" (Luke 14:18-20,*n*).

In this parable, Jesus seems to be alluding to the requirements of the Holy War. In excusing themselves from following the Lord to the heavenly banquet, the people seem to be giving holy reasons, the reasons sanctioned for exemption from the holy war. The exempted persons were freed to do excellent service for the welfare of the whole people. Why then are the people in the parable blamed for not coming to the dinner?

Is it because Jesus is addressing people who rationalize their failure to follow the Lord, by giving holy reasons to excuse themselves from total commitment to him? The parable was indeed addressed to Pharisees who were so zealous for the Law of Moses that they were carefully checking up on Jesus: "They observed him closely" (Luke 14:1,*n*). They were committed people, committed to the law. Unfortunately this holy commitment became unholy, for it impeded them from accepting the Lord Jesus. No reason, however holy, excuses us from accepting the invitation to the heavenly banquet, leaving all things to follow Jesus on the journey to that banquet, and persevering with him in all his trials.

"Blessed is he who shall eat bread in the kingdom of God" (Luke 14:15,*r*). The holy war to win the kingdom and to dine with Jesus in the kingdom requires total renunciation. One must leave his land and his oxen and even his wife, if these stand between him and the Lord. That is, even those nearest and dearest to us must never be allowed to impede our wholehearted following of the Lord to the kingdom.

Elisha found strength for his steadfast journey with Elijah in the sacrificial meal in which he offered his oxen and consecrated himself to his vocation. So the follower of Jesus finds his strength for the journey to the Father's house in the Eucharistic banquet, the sacrificial meal at which we reconsecrate ourselves daily to the following of Christ.

Was Elijah a Celibate?

According to a Jewish tradition, to which St. Ambrose bears witness, (PL 16:192a), Elijah remained a celibate. St. Jerome says that Elijah, Elisha, and many of the brotherhood of the prophets, were celibate (PL 22:408). These Christian writers were celibates themselves, and so they tended to see their own monastic ideals verified in Elijah and in the brotherhood of prophets. They were reading the Scriptures in the light of their own personal situation, and it is legitimate to do this. However, we cannot really show from the Scriptures that Elijah did remain celibate for the sake of the Lord. There is, of course, that Jewish tradition to this effect.

The Scriptures do say that the brotherhood of prophets built a larger dwelling place where they could live with Elisha, their teacher (2 Kings 6:1-2). And with him they ate their meals from a common pot (2 Kings 4:38-41). There is no mention of a woman being among them. Elisha's servant does the cooking, and one of the men cuts up the poisonous gourds into the stew (2 Kings 4:38-39).

If Elijah had a wife, why did he have to be cared for by the widow of Zarephath, or by the ravens in the desert place where he had gone earlier? If he had a wife, why wasn't she there to see him taken up to God? Why wasn't she there to minister to him in his ministry?

Certainly if Elijah had a wife, she must have been one of the most neglected of all wives, because no one ever knew where Elijah was. "The Spirit of the Lord will carry you whither I know not," said the king's servant to him (1 Kings 18:12,r). There is no evidence that the Spirit transported a wife with Elijah wherever he went.

The prophet did have a servant with him when he was running for his life from Jezebel, but even him Elijah dismissed, as he went alone into the solitude of the desert (1 Kings 19:3). Later too he does his best to dismiss Elisha so that he can be alone with the Lord (2 Kings 2). Elijah was a great lover of solitude, and the ancient Christian monks and hermits, and especially the Carmelite friars and nuns later on, took Elijah as one of their models of contemplation. Monks, like Elijah, seek the Lord in purity of heart in the freedom of the desert.

"The Spirit of the Lord will carry you whither I know not." Elijah enjoyed complete mobility in the Holy Spirit because he was so perfectly detached from all ties which could have impeded him. In his purity of heart, his separation from all bonds, he is wholehearted in his attentiveness to the Lord. He stands before the Lord in complete availability. Therefore the Lord can move him freely whenever and wherever he wants him.

He is totally available for the holy war of Yahweh because he has no vineyards to be cultivated, no new house to be established and furnished, no wife to be cherished and knit ever more closely to his heart. He is completely free to be used totally by the Lord. Elisha is like him in this. He burns his plow and sacrifices his oxen so that he can belong totally to the Lord. Like Elijah, he is worth the whole army of Israel's chariots (2 Kings 13:14; 2 Kings 2:11-12). These two are the most mobile of troops in the Lord's war, for in no way are they tied down even by legitimate and holy human concerns for a wife, a house, a vineyard, a farm.

Only Luke's version of the parable of the great dinner has the references to the conditions for the holy war: being free of concern for wife, house, vineyard (Luke 14:16-24; compare Matt. 22:2-10). Because the parable, in Luke, speaks of oxen and plowing, instead of vineyards, it alludes, no doubt, to Elisha who sacrificed his oxen and plow. Luke is continuing his Elijah theme. We can understand why Christian celibates would see themselves in a special way in this parable. They are unimpeded by farms and oxen and concern for a wife and family, and leave all things to follow the Lord. The celibate enjoys Elijah's mobility in the Spirit, for the Lord can use him freely for any of his purposes whatsoever.

In the midst of his people, the Lord needs a light militia of this kind which is easy to maneuver and adapt to every situation. To the true celibate for the Lord, we can say, as the king's servant said to Elijah, "The Spirit of the Lord will carry you whither I know not" (1 Kings 18:12,r).

This, of course, is the ideal of every Christian: to be so free of all impeding attachments to the world that he can be easily led by the Holy Spirit. "All who are led by the Spirit of God are sons of God" (Rom. 8:14,r).

CHAPTER THIRTEEN

ELIJAH, THE PRECURSOR

"I Send My Messenger"

The Lord declared through Malachi, "Lo, I will send you Elijah, the prophet, before the day of the Lord comes, the great and terrible day, to turn the hearts of the fathers to their children, and the hearts of the children to their fathers, lest I come and strike the land with doom" (Mal. 3:23-24,*n*). Elijah will be precursor of the day of the Lord.

A precursor goes before another not just to announce his coming, but also to pave the way for his success. In Christian tradition, John the Baptist is called the precursor of the Lord, because Jesus says that John is the one of whom Malachi wrote: "I send my messenger ahead of you to prepare the way before you" (Matt. 11:10,*n*; compare Mal. 3:1).

The Scriptures apply the title "precursor" only to Jesus himself. The word is used only once in the Scriptures, in the letter to the Hebrews. There Jesus is called "our precursor," the one who has gone before us into heaven, to prepare the way for us: "Like a sure and firm anchor, that hope extends beyond the veil, through which Jesus our *forerunner* has entered on our behalf" (Heb. 6:19-20,*n*, emphasis added).*

If Luke presents both John and Jesus, and also the missionaries sent by Jesus, as new Elijahs or precursors, it is because the figure of Elijah fittingly symbolizes the careers of John, of Jesus, and of the missionaries. Jesus is more fully a

---

Praecursor (Latin); *prodomos* (Greek); forerunner (English).

new Elijah than John is, and the missionaries simply continue
the Lord's own mission as precursor.

John was precursor in preparing the way for the mission of
Jesus. Jesus was precursor because by his journey on the cross
he prepared our way into heaven. He is prefigured by Elijah
taken up in the fiery chariot. The missionaries sent by Jesus
are precursors preparing the Lord's way into the living tem-
ples of human hearts.

Precursor of the Day of the Lord

Sirach repeats Malachi's teaching that Elijah is precursor of
the day of the Lord: "You are destined, it is written, in time to
come to put an end to wrath before the day of the Lord" (Sir.
48:10,n). Before telling us this, Sirach first extols the original
ministry of Elijah, and describes it as a judgment by fire:

Their sinfulness grew more and more,
and they lent themselves to every evil,
till like a fire there appeared the prophet
whose words were as a flaming furnace.
Their staff of bread he shattered,
in his zeal he reduced them to straits;
by God's word he shut up the heavens,
and three times brought down fire.
How awesome are you, Elijah!
Whose glory is equal to yours?
You brought a dead man back to life
from the nether world, by the will of the Lord.
You sent kings down to destruction,
and nobles from their beds of sickness.
You heard threats at Sinai,
at Horeb avenging judgments.
You anointed kings who should inflict vengeance,
and a prophet as your successor.
You were taken aloft in a whirlwind,
in a chariot with fiery horses.
You are destined, it is written, in time to come

to put an end to wrath before the day of the Lord,
to turn back the hearts of fathers toward their sons,
and to re-establish the tribes of Jacob.
Blessed is he who shall have seen you before he dies,
O Elijah, enveloped in the whirlwind (Sir. 47:25—48:12,n).

The ministry of fiery judgment was Elijah's first mission.
But in days to come, Elijah will "put an end to wrath before
the day of the Lord," by turning the hearts of fathers to their
sons, just as on Mount Carmel he had turned Israel's heart
back to God by the fiery sacrifice (1 Kings 18:37).

Sirach modifies Malachi's words slightly. Malachi had said,
"I will send you Elijah . . . to turn the hearts of the fathers to
their children, and the hearts of the children to their fathers"
(3:24n). For Malachi's second phrase, Sirach substitutes a line
from one of Isaiah's Servant poems: "To turn back the hearts of
fathers toward their sons, and to re-establish the tribes of
Jacob" (Sir. 48:10,n).

The Servant's mission, says Isaiah, is "to raise up the tribes
of Jacob" (Isa. 49:6,n). Sirach applies these words to Elijah,
saying that at his second coming he will "re-establish the
tribes of Jacob" (Sir. 48:10). "Raise up" and "re-establish" are
two translations of the word used by Isaiah. Thus Sirach seems
to identify the mission of the Suffering Servant with the mission of Elijah before the day of the Lord.

In substituting "to re-establish the tribes of Jacob" for
Malachi's "to turn the hearts of the children to their fathers,"
Sirach is saying that through conversion of hearts the tribes of
Jacob will be restored. Through conversion, the hearts of the
children of Israel become like the hearts of the patriarchs, "the
first fathers." The hearts of the patriarchs can then "turn to
their children" and recognize and acknowledge them as their
children, for they have now become like their first fathers in
faith and faithfulness.

Third Isaiah had been conscious that neither Abraham nor
Jacob could any longer recognize the Jews as their children, so
far had these gone astray from the ways of God's covenant; and
he appeals to God's fatherly compassion:

> Were Abraham not to know us
>   nor Israel to acknowledge us,
> You, Lord, are our father,
>   our redeemer you are named forever (Isa. 63:16,n).

Sirach, then, seems to identify the new mission of Elijah with the mission of the suffering Servant. Did Jesus think of himself as both New Elijah and Suffering Servant? Did he consider that he was fulfilling Elijah's mission to put an end to wrath before the Day of the Lord?

Certainly Jesus expressed his understanding of his mission partly in terms of the Suffering Servant. But no one image from the Old Testament could adequately express who Jesus was and why he had come. Therefore in expressing who he was and what he was doing, Jesus united all the Old Testament messianic images in a remarkable way, finding in each of them something useful in explaining himself. He is Son of Man, Son of David, Son of God, Suffering Servant, New Elijah, all combined, and infinitely greater. Each figure symbolizes a different aspect of his infinitely rich person and mission.

Did Jesus think of himself in terms of Elijah as precursor? Certainly Luke thinks of Jesus in this way. By casting the fire of the Holy Spirit into the hearts of men by the power of his sacrifice, Jesus converts the hearts of men to God their father and to one another. Thus he puts an end to wrath before the day of the Lord. Let us examine further Luke's presentation of Jesus as precursor.

"The Messenger of the Covenant"

Since the notion of precursor of the Lord is rooted in Malachi's words, the role of the precursor needs to be clarified in the light of Malachi's description of him, and of the work for which he would prepare the way.

> Lo, I am sending my messenger to prepare the way before me;
> And suddenly there will come to the temple
>   the Lord whom you seek

and the messenger of the covenant whom you desire.
Yes, he is coming, says the Lord of hosts (Mal. 3:1,*n*).

"The Lord whom you seek" and "the messenger of the covenant" occur in synonymous parallelism. They are two ways of saying the same thing. "The Lord whom you seek" and "the messenger of the covenant" are one and the same person. Therefore the messenger sent to prepare the way for the coming of "the Lord whom you seek" is not the same person as the messenger of the covenant. The Lord himself is the messenger of the covenant, another messenger prepares his way.

The Hebrew word for messenger is often translated as angel. Angel is an English word derived from the Greek word for messenger. "Angel (or messenger) of the covenant" is a variation of the term "angel (or messenger) of the Lord."

"Angel of the Lord" signified a theophany, a manifestation of God's presence. "The angel of the Lord" is really a presence of God himself, for "the messenger" is the visual form under which God appeared and spoke to men. For example, Yahweh's personal appearance to Moses in the burning bush is called "an angel of the Lord." "There an angel of the Lord appeared to him in fire flaming out of a bush" (Exod. 3:2,*n*). It is clear that this is a presence and manifestation of God himself: "*God* called out to him from the bush, 'Moses, Moses!' " (Exod. 3:4,*n*, emphasis added).

That "the angel of the Lord" is a manifestation of God himself is obvious also in other passages where the expression occurs, for the narratives alternate in referring to it as "the Lord" or as "the angel of the Lord." For example, in the apparitions to Gideon we read, "The *angel* of the Lord appeared to him.... The *Lord* turned to him and said ..." (Judg. 6:12, 14,*n*, emphasis added). Of the visit of Yahweh with Hagar we read, "*The Lord's messenger* found her by a spring in the wilderness ..." (Gen. 16:7,*n*, emphasis added). "To *the Lord* who spoke to her she gave a name, saying, 'You are the God of Vision.' She meant, 'Have I really seen God and remained alive after my vision!' " (Gen. 16:13,*n*, emphasis added).

Malachi's expression, "angel (or messenger) of the covenant" means a presence and manifestation of the God of the covenant, who comes to deal with his covenant people. The Lord announces through Malachi that suddenly he will come in person to the temple and will manifest his presence as "messenger of the covenant." But first he will send his messenger to prepare the way before him.

Jesus, speaking of John the Baptist, says, "It is about this man that Scripture says, 'I send my messenger ahead of you, to prepare your way before you'" (Matt. 11:10,n; compare Mal. 3:1).

If John the Baptist is this messenger who prepares the way, then Jesus is the messenger of the covenant, he is a theophany of God. He is the Lord who comes to his temple, he is God in person present and manifest to his people.

Malachi had written, "Lo, I am sending my messenger to prepare the way before me" (Mal. 3:1,n). In applying them to John, Jesus rephrases the words, for he has heard them as addressed to himself personally: "I send my messenger ahead of you, to prepare your way before you" (Matt. 11:10,n). John the Baptist, Jesus is telling us, is the messenger who prepares the way for Jesus as "angel of the covenant."

Why does the Lord come to his temple?

Lo, I am sending my messenger to prepare the way before
  me.
And suddenly there will come to the temple
the Lord whom you seek
and the messenger of the covenant whom you desire.
Yes, I am coming, says the Lord of hosts.
But who will endure the day of his coming?
And who can stand when he appears?
For he is like the refiner's fire,
or like the fuller's lye.
He will sit refining and purifying silver,
and he will purify the sons of Levi,
refining them like gold or like silver,

that they may offer due sacrifice to the Lord.
Then the sacrifice of Judah and Jerusalem
will please the Lord as in days of old, as in years gone by
(Mal, 3:1-4,n).

The messenger of the covenant, the Lord, will come to his
temple to purify the priests by fire, so that henceforth they will
offer acceptable sacrifice to God. "The messenger of the covenant" is a purifying theophany on a day of the Lord.
The prophet Malachi was very concerned about the holiness of the priesthood and about the purity of the sacrifices
they offered to God in the temple. He reprimands the priests
of his day for the blemished, unacceptable worship which
they were offering to the Lord.

Oh, that one among you would shut the temple gates to
keep you from kindling fire on my altar in vain! I have no
pleasure in you, says the Lord of hosts; neither will I accept
any sacrifice from your hands, for from the rising of the sun,
even to its setting, my name is great among the nations; and
everywhere they bring sacrifice to my name, and a pure
offering (Mal. 1:10-11,n).

These words find their fulfillment only in the Eucharistic
Sacrifice, for this is the only sacrifice offered among all nations, from the rising of the sun even to its setting. It is the
sacrifice of the cross, offered everywhere in the Eucharist. The
messenger of the covenant comes to the temple to purify his
priests and people so that they will be able to offer this acceptable sacrifice.

Luke and Malachi

In his account of the infancy of Jesus, Luke is strongly
influenced by the prophet Malachi. This influence is especially evident in Luke's words concerning John as precursor of
the Lord. Malachi, we said, was concerned about the purification of the priests and of the temple worship. Luke's Gospel

begins in that temple, where a priest, Zechariah, is offering
incense at the hour of the evening sacrifice. Gabriel appears to
tell him he will have a son whom he shall call John. The angel
describes John's mission in Malachi's words concerning the
messenger who prepares the way for the angel of the covenant (Luke 1:16-17).

Later, Zechariah himself, in his canticle, uses the imagery
of Malachi to describe his son's mission: "You will go before
the Lord to prepare his ways" (Luke 1:76,r). Malachi had
promised, a few verses after, that "there will arise the sun of
justice with its healing rays" (Mal. 3:20,n). Zechariah's words,
"the day shall dawn on us from on high" (Luke 1:78,r) are
quite likely a reference to this healing "sun of justice," which
Malachi contrasts with the blazing oven which will burn up
the wicked (Mal. 3:19).

Malachi spoke of "the angel of the covenant." Zechariah
says that Yahweh has remembered his covenant (Luke 1:72)
and has visited his people in mercy (Luke 1:68,78). In this
visit, he is the angel of the covenant, for his visit is a manifestation of his presence, in the person of Christ, the Savior.

Though Zechariah's description of his son's mission (Luke
1:76) is expressed in Malachi's words concerning Elijah (Mal.
3:1-4), the words are abbreviated, and the description brings
out only the tender mercies of the God of the covenant: "He
has dealt mercifully with our fathers, and remembered the
holy covenant he made" (Luke 1:78,n).

John's message as expressed by Zechariah and Gabriel is
really the gospel message. Not a word about an oven burning
the chaff, but only the faithfulness of God to his covenant and
the restoration of his people in holiness and justice (Luke
1:72-75); and the return of "the rebellious to the wisdom of the
just" (Luke 1:17,n). This last phrase is Luke's substitution for
Malachi's words "to turn the hearts of the children to their
fathers" (Mal. 3:24 and Luke 1:17), and for Sirach's words "to
re-establish the tribes of Jacob" (Sir. 48:10,n).

Such is the message preached by the seventy disciples; that
is, all who go forth in the Spirit and power of Jesus, the New
Elijah. Thus Zechariah's words present John the Baptist as a

prefiguring of the Christian preachers who go before the Lord
Jesus to prepare his way into the hearts of men.

The Lord's Presentation in the Temple

In the liturgy for the feast of the Lord's presentation, cele-
brating the coming of Jesus to the Temple at the age of forty
days, the passage from Malachi which we have been considering (3:1-4) is read along with Luke's account of the
presentation (Luke 2:22-40).

Because of the unmistakeable references to the Book of
Malachi in Luke's account of the Lord's infancy, the liturgy
of the Church is correct in using the reading from Malachi to
throw light on the story of the Lord's presentation in the
Temple. Luke is consciously thinking of Malachi's words
when he tells us how the Infant Lord comes to the Temple
in the arms of his mother: "Suddenly there will come to the
Temple the Lord whom you seek!" (Mal. 3:1, *n*).

To understand Luke's account of the presentation we must
realize that it is the climax of his whole story of the Lord's
infancy. Everything in that story leads up to the Lord's coming
to the temple as a child in his mother's arms. The story of the
infancy is a prefiguring of Jesus' whole life and mission. For
Luke presents the Lord's life as his journey up to Jerusalem,
where he goes to the Father's house, the heavenly temple, by
way of the cross. Thus Luke's story of the Lord's infancy is an
interpretation of the Lord's whole life. His coming to the
temple in his mother's arms is symbolic of his life's work as
"angel of the covenant," purifying mankind, like gold in the
fire, in the sacrifice of the cross. Through this sacrifice, which
is offered to God from the rising of the sun to its setting, all of
us can go to the Father's house.

On Mount Horeb Elijah was told that God would purify his
people in the fire of judgment brought upon them through the
swords of Hazael and Jehu (1 Kings 19:15-18). The sword that
pierces Mary's heart, predicted by Simeon at the presentation,
signifies more than the sorrow she suffers as she shares in the
Lord's passion. Mary herself symbolizes God's people as

purified by the Lord's suffering, through their sharing in this suffering. Their sufferings, united with his, are no longer a penalty for sin, but have been changed into a purifying blessing.

The Cleansing of the Temple

The life-mission of Jesus as "angel of the covenant" is foreshadowed in the presentation. It is symbolized likewise in the story of Jesus driving the traders out of the temple (Luke 19:45-48). In his anger on this occasion, Jesus manifests the fiery zeal of Elijah (John 2:17), who purified the worship of Yahweh of all contamination by false worship. His action in clearing the temple of the traders is a parable in action, expressing the meaning of his work on the cross. By his sacrifice, he purifies God's people in his blood, to be the living temple of God's presence.

Perhaps, too, the severity of Jesus on this occasion foreshadows God's judgment on Jerusalem in the year 70 A.D., when the temple was destroyed by the Romans. Jesus, as New Elijah, had come to save his people from this doom, but he had to weep in distress because his mission was rejected. Luke tells the story of the driving out of the traders immediately after telling how Jesus wept over Jerusalem and foretold her destruction (Luke 19:41-44).

Matthew, Mark and John underline the anger of Jesus as he drives the traders from the temple. The gentle Luke says nothing about this anger, and tells only how the Lord wept as he foretold God's judgment upon the temple. Yet, in destroying the temple in the fire of judgment, God is not finished with his people. He will preserve for himself a holy remnant who will welcome the Lord at his coming:

"Your temple will be abandoned. I say to you, you shall not see me until the time comes when you say, 'Blessed is he who comes in the name of the Lord' " (Luke 13:35,n). God's people will once again welcome the Lord, and in receiving him, they themselves will become his living temple.

CHAPTER FOURTEEN

JESUS, THE PRECURSOR

"Elijah Will Restore Everything"

Malachi does not seem to be thinking of the Messiah when he tells how the Lord will send his messenger to prepare for his personal coming to the temple. But the Jewish scribes, reflecting perhaps on Malachi, began to look upon the coming of the Messiah as a day of the Lord, a day of purification of God's people. And they taught that Elijah would return as the Messiah's precursor. Elijah would come to anoint and proclaim the Messiah, just as he had anointed Hazael and Jehu.

Peter, James and John must have been disappointed that this anointing did not take place at the transfiguration, when they saw Elijah conversing with Jesus, along with Moses. Their disappointment would have been all the keener when Jesus told them to keep secret what they had seen on the mountain, until after the Son of Man rose from the dead (Mark 9:9). That is why they ask Jesus, "Why do the scribes say that first Elijah must come?" (Mark 9:11,*r*). This is like saying, "If the scribes say that Elijah will anoint the Messiah, why did Elijah fail to do this when we saw you in glory with him on the mountain? Are the scribes in error?"

In answering, Jesus refers to his passion: "Elijah will indeed come first and *restore everything;* yet why does Scripture say of the Son of Man that he must suffer much and be despised?" (Mark 9:12,*n*, emphasis added). The words that Elijah will come and *restore everything* seem to be a reference to Sirach's words, in which Elijah and the Servant of

Yahweh are identified as the same person (Sir. 48:10; Isa. 49:6).

Jesus here implies that he himself is the New Elijah who will put an end to wrath and restore, not just the tribes of Jacob, but everything. And this work of restoration will be accomplished through his suffering. He says that Elijah will indeed come to restore all things, as the scribes teach, yet why is it that the Scriptures say that the Son of Man must suffer and be despised? The Son of Man is the New Elijah who will restore all things, not by the fiery destruction of the enemies of Israel, but through his sufferings and humiliation.

Thus the words of Jesus are equivalent to: "If I am to perform the fiery purification expected of Elijah, how can it be that, as Son of Man, I must suffer and die?"* Do not be disappointed that Elijah did not anoint and proclaim me on the mountain. I am the one who will restore everything through my death and resurrection.

Later, in his Pentecost sermon, Peter will speak of this restoration of all things by Jesus, the Messiah: "Thus may a season of refreshment be granted you by the Lord when he sends you Jesus, already designated as your Messiah. Jesus must remain in heaven until the time of *universal restoration* which God spoke of long ago through his holy prophets" (Acts 3:20-21,*n*, emphasis added). Thus Peter at Pentecost sees that Jesus is referring to his own second coming when he says, "Elijah will indeed come first and restore everything" (Mark 9:12,*n*). It would seem, then, that Jesus considers himself the New Elijah. And the restoration will be the fruit of his sufferings, for Jesus adds, "Yet why does Scripture say of the Son of Man that he must suffer much and be despised?" (Mark 9:12,*n*).

Though Jesus himself in his sufferings is the New Elijah, in another way John the Baptist, too, fulfills the role of Elijah. Therefore Jesus continues, "Let me assure you, Elijah has already come. They did entirely as they pleased with him, as the Scriptures say of him" (Mark 9:13,*n*). In other words, you

---

*E. J. Mally, Jerome Biblical Commentary on Mark 9:10-13 (JBC 42:56).

were expecting Elijah to anoint and proclaim the Messiah in glorious power. The fact is, John the Baptist is the Messiah's precursor in sufferings. By his own sufferings and death, John has proclaimed the Messiah's sufferings, he has manifested the kind of Messiah you are to expect. "The Son of Man will suffer at their hands in the same way" (Matt. 17:12,*n*).

Precursor into Heaven

After the transfiguration, "Jesus steadfastly set his face to go to Jerusalem" (Luke 9:51). In his journey to the Father's house through the sufferings of the cross, the Lord fulfills the role of angel of the covenant coming to the temple. He is our precursor into the heavenly temple. "Jesus our forerunner has entered beyond the veil on our behalf" (Heb. 6:20,*n*). He has prepared our way into the Father's presence by purifying us on the cross in his own blood.

But Jesus has prepared this way for his people into the heavenly temple by preparing the way for the coming of the Holy Spirit into our hearts. Because he has made the journey to the heavenly temple by way of the cross, he is empowered to send the Holy Spirit into our hearts. Only in the power of the Holy Spirit can we follow Jesus on the way of the cross to the Father in heaven.

In sending the Holy Spirit into our hearts, Jesus cleanses us to be the living temple of the Lord's presence.

"Two and Two before His Face"

When Jesus, the Precursor, is taken up to the Father, he sends the Holy Spirit to clothe his disciples with his own Spirit and authority. In this Spirit and power they go forth as the spiritual heirs of Jesus to prepare the way of the Lord into the hearts of men. "He sent them two and two before his face into every city whither he himself was to come" (Luke 10:1,*d*).

St. Gregory the Great has a magnificent homily on these words of Luke:

Beloved brothers, our Lord and Savior sometimes gives us instruction by words and sometimes by actions. His very deeds are our commands; and whenever he acts silently he is teaching us what we should do. For example, he sends his disciples out to preach two by two, because the precept of charity is twofold—love of God and of one's neighbor.

The Lord sends his disciples out to preach in twos in order to teach us silently that whoever fails in charity toward his neighbor should by no means take upon himself the office of preaching.

Rightly is it said that he sent them ahead of him into every city and place where he himself was to go. For the Lord follows after the preachers, because preaching goes ahead to prepare the way, and then when the words of exhortation have gone ahead and established truth in our minds, the Lord comes to live within us. To those who preach, Isaiah says: Prepare the way of the Lord, make straight the paths of our God. And the psalmist tells them: Make a way for him who rises above the sunset. The Lord rises above the sunset, because from that very place where he slept in death, he rose again and manifested a greater glory. He rises above the sunset because in his resurrection he trampled underfoot the death which he endured. Therefore we make a way for him who rises above the sunset when we preach his glory to you, so that when he himself follows after us, he may illumine you with his love.*

The Two Witnesses

To follow Jesus, our Precursor, into heavenly glory, we his disciples must follow our Precursor to the Jerusalem which puts the prophets to death. "I must go on my way today, and tomorrow, and the day following; for it cannot be that a prophet should perish away from Jerusalem. O Jerusalem,

---

*Homily 17:1-3 (PL 76:1139). Translation from *The Liturgy of the Hours* (New York: The Catholic Book Publishing Company). Used with permission.

Jerusalem, killing the prophets and stoning those who are sent to you!" (Luke 13:33-34,*r*).

The Book of Revelation speaks of two witnesses who are put to death in "the great city ... where their Lord was crucified" (Rev. 11:8,*n*). This is not the geographical, but the symbolic, Jerusalem, which rejects God and his witnesses. It is any place which rejects the Lord and his witnesses.

The two witnesses are probably Peter and Paul, who were martyred in Rome, but they represent all Christian martyrs. The two are described symbolically with the traits of Elijah and Moses, and thus every Christian witness is presented as an Elijah and Moses. "If anyone tries to harm them, fire will come out of the mouths of these witnesses to devour their enemies" (Rev. 11:5,*n*). Their word has all the fire of Elijah's word. The power of their word is irresistable, because the Spirit of Jesus speaks through them.

"These witnesses have the power to close up the sky so that no rain will fall during the time of their mission" (Rev. 11:6,*n*). "I will commission my two witnesses to prophesy for those twelve hundred and sixty days, dressed in sackcloth" (11:3,*n*). The twelve hundred and sixty days equals three and a half years, the length of the drought brought on by the powers of Elijah's word which stopped the rain. "Three and a half years" is a stock symbol in the Scriptures for the brevity of the times of tribulation and of persecution, in contrast with seven, the symbol of wholeness and perfection. Like Elijah's preaching in the time of the drought, their witness is a call to conversion to the true God. The sackcloth they wear, like the hairy mantle of Elijah, symbolizes the call to repentance.

Like Moses, "they also have power to turn water into blood and to afflict the earth at will with any kind of plague" (11:6,*n*). They are empowered to back up their word with signs. Like Elijah, they "stand in the presence of the Lord of the earth" (11:4,*n*). They live in the presence of God, ever ready to serve him by their testimony.

At the end of their mission, they will be slain by the beast. "Their corpses will be in the streets of the great city, which has the symbolic name 'Sodom' [typical of moral perversion] or 'Egypt' [signifying oppression of God's people], where also their Lord was crucified [Jerusalem as symbolic of rejection of God and his Christ]. . . . But after three and a half days, the breath of life which comes from God returned to them" (11:8,11,n). They are taken up to God, just as Jesus and Elijah were: "The two prophets heard a loud voice from heaven say to them, 'Come up here!' So they went up to heaven in a cloud as their enemies looked on" (11:12,n).

Thus described as the new Moses and Elijah, Christian witnesses follow Jesus, their precursor, to the symbolic Jerusalem which kills the prophets. Like Moses and Elijah, who spoke with Jesus at his transfiguration concerning the death he was to undergo in Jerusalem (Luke 9:31), all Christian witnesses testify to the Lord's transfiguration in glory at his resurrection. They give this witness to his glorification by following him to Jerusalem to be crucified. The power of their witness derives from their courageous enduring of martyrdom in the unshaken expectation of being transfigured with him in glory. For their conviction that after their death they will be glorified with him, comes only from their conviction in faith that he has been glorified before them. "He will give a new form to this lowly body of ours and remake it according to the pattern of his glorified body, by his power to subject everything to himself" (Phil. 3:21,n).

CHAPTER FIFTEEN

SEE ELIJAH AND LIVE!

"We Too Shall Have Life!"

Because Elijah was taken up to God in the fiery chariot, a tradition arose among the Jews that Elijah did not die. This gave rise to a hope for salvation from death, a desire to be snatched up to God out of death and sufferings.

This hope seems to be expressed in several of the psalms. "But God will ransom me, from the hand of Sheol will he surely snatch me" (Ps. 49:16,*a*). The word "snatch" is the same Hebrew word which is translated "taken up" in the story of Elijah's assumption in the chariot of fire (2 Kings 2:3,5,9; Sir. 48:9). The word is used also in telling us that Enoch was taken up to God (Gen. 5:24; Sir. 44:16; 49:14; Heb. 11:5-6). The psalmist is expressing his firm conviction that God will take him to himself just as he took Enoch and Elijah. He is stating his belief in "assumption."*

The same word occurs also in Psalm 73:24. "But I will always be with you. Take hold of my right hand, lead me into your council, and with glory *take* me to yourself" (Ps. 73:23-24,*a*, emphasis added). In these verses, the psalmist used terms that allude to the story of the assumption of Enoch in Genesis: "Enoch walked with God, and he was no longer here, for God took him" (5:24,*n*). The psalmist declares that he too will ever be close to God ("I will always be with you")

---

*Mitchell Dahood, *Psalms I* (*The Anchor Bible*, Volume 16; New York: Doubleday, 1966), p. 301.

and will walk with him ("Take hold of my right hand, lead me"). Because he has walked with God, he requests the same privilege that was granted to Enoch and Elijah: "Take me to yourself!"*

Elisha had *seen* Elijah taken up, and that was the sign that he would share in the spirit and power of Elijah. Reflection on this story gave rise among the Jews to a desire to *see* Elijah just as Elisha had seen him:

> Happy shall they be who see you,
> and those who have fallen asleep in love,
> for we too will have life (Sir. 48:11, *j*).

To see Elijah before one dies would be a sign that one would share in Elijah's life with God.

We can understand then why Peter and James and John were so excited when they saw Elijah conversing with Jesus on the mountain of the transfiguration. "Happy shall they be who see you . . . for we too will have life!" Peter wants to live permanently on the mountain with God, along with Moses and Elijah and Jesus: "Master, how good it is for us to be here! Let us set up three booths, one for you, and one for Moses, and one for Elijah" (Luke 9:33,*n*). No doubt Peter expects to live in Jesus' booth as his right hand man, just as later on James and John ask to sit at either side of him in his glory.

But this desire for immortal life is not fulfilled in seeing Elijah. The disciples cannot yet be taken up. Jesus brings them down from the mountain, and speaks of his coming death. In fact, his death was the topic of conversation with Moses and Elijah on the mountain: "They appeared in glory and spoke of his passage which he was about to fulfill in Jerusalem" (Luke 9:31,*n*). Before the disciples can live in permanent communion with God in his heavenly presence, they will have to see Jesus taken up into glory by way of suffering and death on the cross.

Ibid., Psalms II, p. 195. The Jerusalem Bible hesitates to see a reference to Enoch and Elijah in these two psalms.

Sirach's text about seeing Elijah before dying is a very difficult one, because we are uncertain about Sirach's exact words. The Hebrew text is mutilated, and the ancient Greek translations have two variations. Therefore it is hard to determine exactly what Sirach wrote. We shall compare six English translations, some based on the uncertain Hebrew text, others based on the Greek versions.

The scholars who prepared the Jerusalem Bible are convinced that the Greek translation made by Sirach's grandson about 132 B.C. is the text which is divinely inspired by the Holy Spirit. But the scholars who prepared the New American Bible consider that the Hebrew text is the inspired one. The Catholic Church from the beginning has used the Greek version, and thus has seemed to consider that the Greek is the inspired version. The Greek text seems to indicate a belief in immortality which is not found in the Hebrew text.

Clear belief in immortality appeared in Jewish thinking precisely in that period between the writing of the Hebrew text by Sirach, and its translation into Greek by his grandson. That was the period of the Maccabees and the severe persecution by Antiochus Epiphanes. The grandson could have been divinely inspired in his work of translating and modifying his grandfather's text of Sirach 48:11, and under this divine inspiration, he could have brought out more clearly the idea of immortal life with God. In any case, the Greek text seems to bear witness to Jewish hope for life with God after death.

Let us examine various English versions of Sirach 48:11.

Happy shall they be who see you
and those who have fallen asleep in love;
for we too will have life. (Jerusalem Bible)

Happy are those who saw you
and those who fell asleep in love,
for we will surely live. (Chicago)

Blessed is he who shall have seen you
before he dies. (New American)

Blessed are those who saw you
and were honored with your love
(for we also shall certainly live). (New English)

Blessed are they that saw thee
and were honored with thy friendship.
For we live only in our life,
but after death our name shall not be such. (Douay)

Blessed are those who saw you
and those who have been adorned in love,
for we also shall surely live. (Revised Standard)

All these translations are agreed that it is a blessing to see
Elijah. But they do not seem to agree on the nature of that
blessing.

There is a disagreement about one of the words of Sirach.
Three translations render the word as "fall asleep" or "die"
(j,n,Chicago): "Blessed is he who shall have seen you before
he dies" (n). The other three translate the word as "honored"
or "adorned" (d,r,e): "Blessed are those who were honored
with your friendship (or love)."

Does the verse refer to death, or does it refer to love of God,
or to friendship with Elijah? The answer to this would give
also the answer to the question, "What is the blessing one
receives in seeing Elijah?"

The Douay version says that the blessing is friendship with
Elijah. This translation also seems to rule out hope of an
afterlife: "for we live only in our life, but after death our name
shall not be such." The Douay version was based on an old
Latin translation, which, in turn, was made, not from the inspired Greek of Sirach's grandson, but from a secondary Greek
version. Like the Hebrew, this version expresses no hope of
an afterlife. At most, it offers some vague hope that through
friendship with Elijah, who did not die, one can escape from
the fact that "we live only in our life". In older Hebrew
thinking, "the shades" in Sheol were but shadows of their
former selves, so weak and lifeless that they had no name or

personality. Maybe through friendship with this man who was taken up to God, we can have a name after death—a real life, a personality.

The translations which are based on the Greek version speak of death, of love, and of life. To live, one must see Elijah and die in love. The translations which take into account the Greek of Sirach's grandson (*j,r,e,* Chicago) agree that the blessing which one receives in seeing Elijah is life with God, not just friendship with Elijah.

The New American Bible is based exclusively on the Hebrew text, and does not say what the blessing is. It says simply, "Blessed is he who shall have seen you before he dies." This translation omits the reference to life which is found in the Greek. But since it is a blessing to see Elijah before one dies, what would this blessing be, if not life after death? Surely if everything ends with death, to see even a great hero of Hebrew history at that moment would not in itself be much of a fulfillment or blessing. "If our hopes in Christ are limited to this life only we are the most pitiable of men" (1 Cor. 15:19,*n*). However, since this great hero Elijah did not die, but was taken up to God, would not the blessing of seeing him somehow imply that, like him, one would be taken up? Thus, the desire to see Elijah is a desire to live where he is, with God.

When Jesus was dying on the cross, he cried out, "Eli, Eli, lema sabachtani," that is, "My God, my God, why have you forsaken me?" Some of the bystanders thought that he was calling upon Elijah, and said, "Let's see whether Elijah comes to his rescue" (Matt. 27:46-49,*n*)

The thought that Elijah might come to rescue Jesus may have been influenced by Sirach's words that one is blessed in seeing Elijah before one dies. Did these bystanders think that perhaps the dying Jesus would see Elijah, who would save him from death?

But the dying Jesus did not see Elijah. "Jesus cried out in a loud voice, and gave up his spirit" (Matt. 27:50,*n*). It is not Elijah whom we must see if we wish to have immortal life with God. We must see Jesus, not rescued from death by Elijah, not saved from death by his Father, but taken up to

God out of death itself. Jesus had to die, that we might live by the power of his resurrection.

Simeon Sees the Lord's Anointed

Does Luke's theme of seeing Jesus as the New Elijah show up in his story of the infancy of Jesus? In the story of the presentation of the infant Jesus in the Temple, Simeon sees Jesus, the Lord's Anointed, and therefore he can die in peace:

> There lived in Jerusalem at the time a certain man named Simeon. He was just and pious, and awaited the consolation of Israel, and the Holy Spirit was upon him. It was revealed to him by the Holy Spirit that he would not experience death until he had seen the Anointed of the Lord (Luke 2:25-26,n).

In writing this, was Luke once again consciously presenting Jesus, the Lord's Anointed, as the New Elijah? Was he thinking of Sirach's words that one is blessed in seeing Elijah before one dies?

After Simeon sees the Messiah and takes him into his arms, he sings his canticle, saying that now he can die in peace, for his eyes have witnessed God's salvation:

> Now let your bond servant depart in peace, Lord, in agreement with your word, for my eyes have seen your salvation, which you have prepared before all the nations, a light for revelation to the Gentiles, and a glory to your people Israel (Luke 2:29-32,m).

Simeon's words echo the words addressed to the Servant of Yahweh in Isaiah: "I will make you a light to the nations, that my salvation may reach to the ends of the earth" (Isa. 49:6,n). Simeon is saying that Jesus is the Servant of Yahweh, light of the nations.

Simeon sings in this way because he has seen Jesus, the Lord's Anointed. He sees God's salvation in the person of

Jesus. Therefore Luke may be thinking of Sirach 48:11 as well as of Isaiah 49:6. We have already noted how Sirach 48:10 combines the figure of Elijah and the figure of the Suffering Servant. The following verse in Sirach speaks of the blessing found in seeing Elijah before dying.

When Luke tells us at the end of his Gospel that the disciples saw Jesus taken up to God, this is the sign that they are clothed with the power of the Holy Spirit to share in the Lord's mission. This is the mission to prepare the way for God to come into the living temple, the hearts of his people. Simeon, seeing the Lord's Anointed in the temple in Jerusalem, is not blessed by sharing in the preaching mission of the disciples, because he dies in peace after seeing the infant Jesus. His blessing, rather, is the peaceful hope of eternal life with Jesus, the New Elijah. He can die in hope, for the Lord has arrived in his temple to accomplish his saving work.

On second thought, Simeon does receive the Holy Spirit to share in the preaching mission, for his very words, which we have been considering, are preaching that will be heard till the end of time.

Luke's story of the coming of the Lord Jesus to the temple in his infancy is an interpretation of the whole career of Jesus. The life work of Jesus, as Luke expresses it in this story, is to come to his temple and purify it to be the dwelling place of God, where he will be fittingly worshipped by the offering of a pure sacrifice. And the temple is his people. But to dwell in God's temple and to offer him fitting worship is to share God's life with him, it is to live in communion with him. However, only through the death of Jesus can we be taken up to God in glory and have this communion with him. Therefore Simeon can die in peace, for he has seen Jesus, the Lord's Anointed, who has come to die and to be taken up into glory.

Since Luke's account of the presentation is an interpretation of the Lord's whole career, Simeon is a prefiguring of all of us. Simeon sees God's salvation in the person of Jesus; we, in faith, see Jesus in his life's journey up to Jerusalem, where he is taken up to God in his death on the cross. Simeon's prophecy certainly refers to the Lord's death: "This child is destined to be the downfall and the rise of many in Israel, a sign that will be opposed" (Luke 2:34,n).

Simeon sees Jesus, the Anointed, in reality. And in prophecy, he sees the work to be accomplished by Jesus in his death and resurrection. He sees the whole career of Jesus, who has come to die so that we might die with him in peace, and come to the glory of the resurrection.

What Simeon sees in prophecy, we are to see in the reality as it has been accomplished by Jesus. We are to see the Suffering Servant, the New Elijah, taken up to God in his death on the cross.

Blessed shall we be who see you, O Jesus, the New Elijah, and have fallen asleep in love, for we too shall have life!

"Will Not Taste Death"

Perhaps Sirach's words, "Blessed is he who shall have seen you before he dies" (Sir. 48:11,n), throw light on the difficult Gospel text, "I assure you, there are some standing here who will not taste death until they see the reign of God" (Luke 9:27,n). That is, the reign of God will be established before you die, and some of you will see it.

Perhaps the saying has the more profound meaning that they will not die, because in faith they will see Jesus in the glory of his reign. It is not a case of not dying physically, but of having eternal life, because in faith they have seen the Lord taken up in glory. For in the very next incident in all three synoptic gospels, Peter, James and John see Jesus in the glory of the transfiguration. "They saw his glory," says Luke (9:32). The story of the transfiguration just after the words, "Some standing here will not taste death until they see the reign of God," implies that these words find at least a partial fulfillment in the transfiguration.

In seeing the Lord's glory in the transfiguration, the disciples see the reign of God already operative. The transfiguration is an anticipation of what they will see in the Lord's ascension, when they will see him taken up in glory. Seeing the transfigured and ascended Lord in faith is certainly a pledge of eternal life for the believer, "who will not taste death" (Luke 9:27); just as Simeon received a pledge of immortal life from the Spirit in the promise that he would not taste death until he had seen the Lord's Anointed. The believer can therefore address Jesus in the words which Sirach addressed to Elijah, "Blessed is he who shall have seen you before he dies!" (Sir. 48:11,n).

"Blessed are the eyes that see what you see. I tell you, many prophets and kings wished to see what you see but did not see it, and to hear what you hear, but did not hear it" (Luke 10:23-24,n). You are blessed in seeing the accomplishment of all that the prophets hoped for. You see God's Anointed One, and you see God's salvation in his life and person.

"A Hard Saying"

In John's Gospel, too, seeing the Son of Man taken up to God in the ascension is a pledge of eternal life. This life is granted to us in the Eucharist: "What if you were to see the Son of Man ascending where he was before?" (John 6:63,r).

Jesus said this in response to the complaint of some of his disciples that his words about the Bread of Life are a "hard saying" (John 6:60):

Many of his disciples when they heard it, said, "This is a hard saying; who can listen to it?" But Jesus, knowing in himself that his disciples murmured at it, said to them, "Do you take offense at this? Then what if you were to see the Son of Man ascending where he was before? (John 6:60-62,r).

We wonder whether the words "hard saying" in John's telling of this incident are a reference back to Elijah's words to Elisha, "You have asked a hard thing" in asking for a double portion of my spirit. "Still, if you see me taken up from you, your wish will be granted" (2 Kings 2:10,n). When the disciples say that our Lord's words about the eucharistic Bread of

Life are a hard saying which they cannot accept, Jesus replies, "Do you take offense at this? Then what if you were to see the Son of Man ascending where he was before?"

To see the Son of Man ascending in glory is the sign for us that he truly is our Bread of Life which has come down from heaven, the Bread which nourishes us in the paschal mystery of his death and resurrection. Only when in faith we see him as Son of God ascending in glory to where he came from are we able to accept the reality of the eucharistic bread and cup, in which we eat the Body of the risen Lord and drink his Blood. In the eucharistic celebration, we are to see the paschal mystery operative: the mystery of the Lord's being lifted up on the cross and exalted in glory and sending the Holy Spirit. This is the reality commemorated in the Eucharist, this is the reality which nourishes us with eternal life in the eucharistic Bread of Life.

Elisha's "hard request" for the spirit was granted when he saw the assumption of Elijah. Shall we not therefore hope for the life-giving Spirit when we "see" the risen and ascended Lord in the Eucharist, and eat him as our Bread of Life who was taken up to where he came from? "What if you were to see the Son of Man ascending to where he was before?" (John 6:62,*r*).

In John's Gospel, the return of Jesus to the Father in the paschal sacrifice is not presented as his being taken up, but as ascending by his own glorious power: "I am ascending to my Father and your Father, to my God and your God" (John 20:17,*r*). "No one has ascended into heaven, but he who descended from heaven, the Son of Man" (John 3:13,*r*). His next words to Nicodemus show that his ascension to the Father is one and the same movement as his being lifted up on the cross: "As Moses lifted up the serpent in the wilderness, so must the Son of Man be lifted up" (John 3:14,*r*). His ascension to the Father in being lifted up on the cross is the sign that he is the one who gives the new birth in water and the Spirit (John 3:5). We who in faith see him lifted up shall live, for we receive the Holy Spirit, as Elisha received Elijah's spirit when he saw him taken up.

The first Elijah did not know at first whether he could concede the hard request of his eager disciple. Jesus definitely promises the hard thing to those who are willing to believe and receive it.

"Lord, That I May See!"

Seeing Jesus taken up to heaven as the New Elijah is the pledge that we will receive the Spirit of Jesus, giving us power for our journey to the Father and for our mission to our fellowmen. But we must not forget that seeing him ascend includes seeing him lifted up on the cross. We must see Jesus in his sufferings as well as in his glory. The successful journey of Jesus to the Father does not remove the necessity of making the bitter journey of the cross with him.

Is not that the meaning which Luke attaches to the prayer of the blind man of Jericho, in the course of our Lord's journey up to Jerusalem: "Lord, that I may see!" (Luke 18:41,c). Jesus had just foretold his passion. " 'Behold, we are going up to Jerusalem, and everything that is written of the Son of Man by the prophets will be accomplished. For he will be delivered up to the Gentiles, and will be mocked and shamefully treated and spit upon; and they will scourge him and kill him, and on the third day he will rise.' But they understood none of these things; this saying was hid from them, and they did not grasp what was said" (Luke 18:31-34,r).

Immediately after these words about the spiritual blindness of the disciples, Luke tells the story of the blind man and his prayer, "Lord, that I may see!" The disciples were unable to see the need for a suffering Messiah. Luke is hinting that we, too, should pray, "Lord, that I may see!" That I may see the place of the cross in my life!

The disciples did not see the need of the cross till they had seen Jesus in the glory of his resurrection. It is the glorious Jesus who is so insistent on the need of following him in the way of the cross: "Did not Christ have to suffer these things before entering into his glory?" (Luke 24:26,c). Luke alone reports this saying of Jesus. He is the evangelist who more clearly than the others highlights the necessity of making the journey of the cross with Jesus. One dines with Jesus in the Kingdom only if one perseveres with him in his trials. Lord, may I see you taken up! Your being taken up in glory is one same movement with your being lifted up on the cross. And so it is with me, your disciple!

CHAPTER SIXTEEN

WHAT THEY SAW ON CALVARY

Elijah had prayed on Mount Carmel that God would turn back the hearts of the people to himself (1 Kings 18:37). The prayer was answered by the grace of faithfulness given to the seven thousand who did not bend their knees to Baal. Elijah was God's servant in this work of turning his people's hearts back to himself.

The prophet did not see the fruitfulness of his work while it was still in progress. The fruit was not manifested until Elijah had been taken up. Indeed, only during the fiery trials sent upon Israel after Elijah had gone forth from this earth did the fruit develop. "The saying holds true, 'One sows and another reaps'" (John 4:37,r). The Lord's laborers who see little fruit for their efforts should know that someone else will reap the harvest for the Lord.

Later generations so clearly saw the fruitfulness of Elijah's work that Malachi and Sirach expected the return of Elijah before the day of the Lord, once again to turn the hearts of the people back to God.

No doubt this expectation of Elijah's return developed from a strong sense of Elijah's continuing power of intercession for God's people. After all, if Elijah was taken up in a fiery chariot to God's own throne, then he was with the Lord to intercede for his people. He was continuing the intercession he had begun on Mount Carmel and Mount Sinai. As God had received his intercession on Sinai and had responded by sending Elijah forth again on his mission, so no doubt he would receive his heavenly intercession and would send him forth once again to convert the hearts of God's people in the last days.

Therefore, speaking the word of the Lord, Malachi promises a return of Elijah:

> Behold, I will send you Elijah the prophet before the great and terrible day of the Lord comes, and he will turn the hearts of fathers to their children, and the hearts of children to their fathers, lest I come and smite the land with a curse (Mal. 4:5,*r*).

Here the conversion to be brought about by Elijah is presented in terms of reconciliation among God's people. But this is not surprising, for the covenant of God with his people is a covenant uniting the people among themselves as God's own family. A people divided among themselves can be reconciled with God only by being reconciled among themselves.

Sirach repeats Malachi's expectation of Elijah's new mission of conversion of hearts:

> You are destined, it is written, in time to come to put an end to wrath before the day of the Lord, to turn back the hearts of fathers toward their sons, and to reestablish the tribes of Jacob (Sir. 48:10,*n*).

Sirach's words echo not only Elijah's prayer that God will turn his people's hearts back to himself (1 Kings 18:37). They echo also Isaiah's second Servant poem. It is the Servant's mission to bring back Jacob to Yahweh (Isa. 49:5), and to restore to him the remnant of Israel (Isa. 49:6). The mission of Elijah before the Day of the Lord is thus identified by Sirach with the mission of the Servant of Yahweh.

Little do Malachi and Sirach realize that God's promise to send Elijah again will be fulfilled in a way gloriously surpassing all they could have expected. The Elijah sent again would, in reality, be the Son of God, Jesus, the New Elijah.

In the annunciation to Zechariah, Gabriel announces the

mission of John the Baptist in the terms used by Malachi and Sirach, but states more explicitly that the conversion of God's people in reconciliation with one another is also their conversion to God:

> He will be filled with the Holy Spirit even from his mother's womb. And he will turn many of the sons of Israel to the Lord their God, and he will go before him in the Spirit and power of Elijah to turn the hearts of the fathers to the children, and the disobedient to the wisdom of the just, to make ready for the Lord a people prepared (Luke 1:15-17,r).

But John the Baptist, too, will be a new Elijah only in a partial way. He will decrease before the Lord Jesus, who alone can bring to fulfillment what Elijah and John began by way of preparation for him. Only in Jesus can the reconciliation be accomplished. "God was in Christ reconciling the world to himself" (2 Cor. 5:19,r).

The Cross and the Conversion of Hearts

When Elijah prayed on Mount Carmel that God would send fire from heaven to consume the sacrifice, he asked the fire as a sign manifesting Yahweh as the true God, and as a sign also that God himself had turned his people's hearts back to him (1 Kings 18:37). Conversion and reconciliation is God's own work in the hearts of his people. He is the one who both begins and completes the work of covenant renewal. He is a God who seeks out his people before they seek him. We think of the words of John of the Cross, that great disciple of Elijah: If a person is seeking God, it is only because God is seeking that person still more.

Elijah prayed, then, that the sacrifice he prepared on Mount Carmel would turn the hearts of Israel back to God. But the sacrifice consumed by the fire from heaven was only the beginning of a process of conversion which took time to complete, and was finished only after Elijah had gone from this earth. So too Luke shows a similar process of conversion which begins when Jesus offers himself in the sacrifice of the cross on Mount Calvary. The process begun on Calvary is completed only on Pentecost when Jesus pours out from heaven the fire of the Holy Spirit as the fruit of his sacrifice.

Let us trace this thought in Luke's twofold work, his Gospel and the Acts of the Apostles.

The theme of "seeing" Elijah taken up seems to be continued by Luke in his story of the Lord's crucifixion. The work of conversion begins in the hearts of the people looking on at Calvary, when they see Jesus lifted up on the cross. "And all the multitudes who assembled to see the sight, when they *saw* what had taken place, returned home beating their breasts" (Luke 23:48,*r*, emphasis added).

In his account of the crucifixion, Luke brings out the power of the sacrifice of Jesus to bring about the conversion of hearts. Those who *see* the Lord taken up on the cross are moved to repentance.

The *seeing* of Jesus on the cross is no mere disinterested looking on, still less is it idle curiosity in a cruel spectacle. It is true contemplation of a divine mystery. On the hill of Calvary there are present not just mockers and spitters and enemies of Jesus. His friends are there too, especially his women disciples. "All his friends and the women who had accompanied him from Galilee were standing at a distance watching everything" (Luke 23:49,*n*).

The "seeing" or watching is not just an idle looking on; it is an increasing involvement of heart with Jesus. There is already an involvement on the part of the women even before they see what takes place in the crucifixion. For they have been following Jesus on his journey all the way from Galilee. They have made the way of the cross. Therefore their hearts are open to receive the cross's power to complete the conversion of their hearts.

The daughters of Jerusalem, too, who weep for Jesus along the way of the cross, have some sort of openness to Jesus. Their human compassion, which makes them weep for the suffering Jesus, opens them to God's compassion. Jesus opens them still more so that they will be able to experience the power of his sufferings to bring about their conversion. He appeals to them to let this conversion be accomplished in them and to let God's compassion work in them. "Daughters of Jerusalem, do not weep for me, but weep for yourselves and for your children" (Luke 23:28,*r*). He calls for the repentance which will open them to the power of the cross.

Not only "the daughters of Jerusalem" and the women who followed him from Galilee, but even the great crowds who have assembled at the cross, are touched by what they see. The process of conversion begins in their hearts: "And all the multitudes who assembled to see the sight, when they saw what had taken place, returned home beating their breasts" (Luke 23:48,*r*).

But it is only on Pentecost that their incipient conversion takes full effect and bears its fruits. When Peter preaches to the assembled crowds on Pentecost, he puts before their eyes once again the crucified and risen Lord who has been taken up into glory: "This is the Jesus God has raised up, and we are his witnesses. Exalted at God's right hand, he first received the promised Holy Spirit from the Father, then poured this Spirit out on us" (Acts 2:32-33,*n*).

"Now when they heard this, they were cut to the heart, and said to Peter and the rest of the apostles, 'Brethren, what shall we do?' And Peter said to them, 'Repent and be baptized, every one of you, in the name of Jesus Christ for the forgiveness of your sins; and you shall receive the gift of the Holy Spirit" (Acts 2:37-38,*r*).

Hearts were already being affected on Calvary, and the people returned home beating their breasts. At Pentecost the people are "cut to the heart." They repent, are baptized, and receive the Holy Spirit, and the work of conversion is completed. For only in the fire of love kindled in hearts by the Holy Spirit can a sinner effectively turn back completely to God. This work of the Holy Spirit in hearts is the fruit of the Lord's being "taken up" to the Father on the cross.

Thus the work of Jesus in converting hearts to God parallels that of the first Elijah. Hearts were affected on Mount Carmel

when Elijah's prayer brought fire from heaven upon the sacrifice he had prepared, but the full effect of the conversion
came about only in the purifying trials of the people which
came later. The seven thousand who proved faithful to
Yahweh in the trials were the fruit of what Yahweh and Elijah
had begun on Mount Carmel. So too all Christian conversion
is the fruit of the sacrifice of Jesus who was consumed in the
fire of love poured out upon him for all of us.

The Lord's missionaries and ministers should recognize a
similar pattern in their own work. The fruits of conversion take
time to develop in hearts, and missionaries should not be
discouraged if the fruit of their labors is not always immediately evident. The sacrificial labors of the missionary are
a sharing in the Lord's own sacrifice on the cross. Missionary
labors are fruitful only to the extent that they are carried out in
union with the crucified Lord, "the Living One" (Luke
24:5,n).

Seeing the "Just Man"

The women who followed Jesus from Galilee to Calvary
and the crowds assembled at the cross are not the only ones
who "saw these things" and experienced the power of the
crucified Jesus to convert hearts. The centurion is mentioned
first. "Now when the centurion saw what had taken place, he
praised God and said, 'Truly this was a just man!'" (Luke
23:47,c). Surely this centurion was open to receive the Holy
Spirit in all his fullness at Pentecost, so that his Christian
conversion would be complete.

What the centurion saw was not just the physical death of
Jesus. The sight that moved his heart was the attitude of Jesus
toward his Father: "Jesus, crying with a loud voice, said,
'Father, into thy hands I commend my spirit!'" (Luke
23:46,r). He saw also Jesus' attitude of forgiveness: "Father,
forgive them, for they know not what they do" (23:34,r). He
saw him receive the repentant thief into his Father's love:
"Truly, I say to you, today you will be with me in Paradise"
(23:43,r).

It is not enough, then, to see Jesus "taken up" in the glory of the Ascension. Like the centurion, we need to see Jesus going to the Father in filial surrender and loving obedience: "Father, into thy hands I commend my spirit!" The "just man" Jesus, more than John the Baptist, is the one who turns "the disobedient to the wisdom of the just" (Luke 1:17,*r*). For only the fire of the Holy Spirit, poured out by Jesus into the hearts of the repentant, can turn the disobedience of sin into loving obedience to the Father.

Those who stand at the cross and see these things are moved to the heart. They are ready for the outpouring of the Holy Spirit of love and the completion of their Christian conversion. In writing these things in the way that he did, it is Luke's intention that we too, his readers, "see what has taken place," so that our hearts too will be converted. Luke intends to get his readers fully involved in the mystery of Christ which he presents.

He wants us to see what the centurion saw, what the crowds who were moved to beat their breast saw. He wants us to be present, with the women "who saw the tomb and how his body was laid" (23:55,*r*), when Jesus is buried. He wants us to be with these women on the morning of his resurrection when they see the empty tomb (Luke 24:1-3), and then in faith see "the Living One" (24:5,*n*).

He wants us to see the Lord "in the breaking of the bread" with the disciples of Emmaus (Luke 24:35). "And their eyes were opened and they recognized him" (24:31,*r*). He wants us to be there, looking on with faith, when Jesus says to the disciples on the night of his resurrection, "See my hands and my feet, that it is I myself" (24:39,*r*).

In short, he would have us see the New Elijah in his whole movement through death to glory, his whole journey home to his Father's house. Only if we see him "taken up" in this full meaning of "taken up," will we be clothed in his Spirit and power. We must not only see all this in faith. We must become involved in it all, so that we can live and experience it with the Lord.

INDEX OF SCRIPTURE REFERENCES

Genesis	page
2:23	88
3:8	43
5:24	113
10	12
16:7-13	101
17:1	31

Exodus	
3:2-4	101
3:6	41
19:18-19	42
24:1-2	41
33:18-23	42
34:7	50
40:34-38	24

Leviticus	
16:2	41
25:5	87

Numbers	
11:17-29	11

Deuteronomy	
6:4-5	31
12:11	24
18:13	31
20:2-8	91-92
21:17	7
24:5	92
32:39	22

Judges	
6:12-14	101

Ruth	
3:9	87

1 Samuel	
18:4	87

1 Kings	page
17:1	15-18,30
17:8-24	18-21
17:12	19
17:19-22	21
17:21	39
17:23	20,39
17:24	20,21
18:1-40	32
18:1	23,32
18:12	23,95-96
18:21-24	29
18:21	29,48
18:22	52
18:26-29	26
18:27	33
18:36	33-34,36
18:37	33-34,39,49, 99,125-127
18:38-40	17
18:38	72
18:39	48
18:42	55
19:1-18	6
19:1-4	39
19:3	95
19:4	40
19:8	78
19:9-10	45
19:9	40,43
19:10	30,35,45-46,49, 52,59,61,91
19:11-13	42-43
19:12	43,62
19:13	41
19:14	45,46
19:15-18	48,66,107
19:17	91
19:18	46
19:19-21	81-84
19:19	85-89

2 Kings	page
1:8	85
1:9-12	65-66
1:10	17,66
1:12	17
2:1-18	5-8,23-24
2:2-6	13,80,95
2:3,5,9	113
2:9-12	5
2:9	5
2:10	8,55,121
2:12	8,25
2:13-14	86
2:15	8
2:16	24
3:11	82
4:8-37	20
4:29	69
4:33-35	21
4:38-39	95
4:38-41	9, 95
4:42-44	9
6:1-7	9,95
8:7-12	48
9:1-10	48
9:13	87
13:14	96

Job	
19:25	87

Psalms	
19:14	87
49:16	113
73:23-24	113
104:1	89
104:3	9
123:2	17

Wisdom	
16:13	22

Sirach	
44:16	113
47:25-48:12	98-99
48:9	113
48:10	55,98-99,104, 107-108,119, 126

Sirach	page
48:11	7,114-118, 119-121
49:14	113
50	56
50:1-5	56
50:19-20	57
50:21	57

Isaiah	
6:5	41
6:6-7	42
19:1	9,24
33:14-16	41
41:14	87,88
49:5	126
49:6	99,108,118-119, 126
61:2	68
63:16	88,99-100

Jeremiah	
7:1-15	25
30:21	41,60

Ezekiel	
1	9
1:4	24
1:12	24
10	9
10:18-23	25
10:20	24
16:8	88
16:14	89

Daniel	
7:9	24

Hosea	
6:5	91

Zechariah	
13:4	85

Malachi	
1:10-11	103
3:1-4	100-105

Malachi	page
3:1	11,66,97
3:19-20	104
3:23-24	55,66,68,97,
(4:5-6)	99,104,126

Matthew	
3:4	86
10:1-5	12
10:41-42	19
11:7-9	86
11:10	97,102
16:18	31
16:24	30
17:12	109
22:2-10	96
24:28	16
26:31	53
27:46-49	117
27:49	55
27:50	117

Mark	
3:14	83
6:7-13	12
6:18	86
9:3	89
9:9-13	107-108
16:6	80

Luke	
1:13-17	10-11,104,127
1:17	104,131
1:68	22,104
1:72	104
1:76	104
1:78	22,104
2:22-40	105-106
2:25-26	118
2:29-32	118
2:34	119-120
2:41	76
2:49	6,76
3:16-17	67
3:21-22	26
4:1-21	26
4:18-19	68

Luke	page
6:12	27
7:11-17	20-22
7:16	20-21,66
8:52,55	21
9:20	27
9:23	64
9:27	120-121
9:28	27
9:29	71
9:30	66
9:31	71,112,114
9:32	120
9:33	114
9:51-55	65-66
9:51	5,52,71,75,109
9:52	11
9:54	17-18,66
9:56	66-67
9:57-58	76-79
9:59-60	79-81
9:61-62	81-84
10:1	10-11,12,109
10:2	69
10:4	69
10:21-22	27,69-70
10:23-24	121
11:23	71
12:49	63,67,70
12:50	63,67
12:51	71
13:22	71
13:33-34	110-111
13:35	106
14:1	94
14:15	94
14:16-24	93-94,96
14:25	75
18:31-41	123
19:36-38	87
19:41-44	106
19:45-48	106
21:3-4	19
22:15-16	70,72,76
22:28-30	64,93
22:32	31
22:39-43	51

Luke	page
22:40,46	64
23:28	129
23:34	54,62,130
23:43	130
23:46	130
23:47	130
23:48-49	128-129
23:55	131
24:1-3	131
24:5-6	20,80
24:5	130
24:26	6,52,123
24:31	131
24:35-39	131
24:44-45	79
24:49	9,10,88
24:50-51	5,52,56
24:52	57

John	
2:17	106
3:3	53
3:5	53,122
3:13	53,122
3:14	122
4:37	125
5:25	21-22
6:57	14
6:60-63	121-122
11:11	21
11:43-44	21
13:36	53
14:1-5	53,76
14:16	55-56
16:32	53
20:17	122
20:28	36
21:19	53

Acts	
1:1-8	79
1:9	9
1:13-15	10
2:1-4	10
2:14-21	12
2:32-33	129
2:33	27,57

Acts	page
2:37-38	129
2:38,41	12
3:20-21	108
8:39	27
16:6-10	27

Romans	
5:5	37
8:9	27
8:14	27,96
8:26-27	34
8:33	46
11:2-5	46-47
14:4-5	46

1 Corinthians	
7:5	86-87
15:19	117

2 Corinthians	
4:10	64
5:19	127
12:9-10	44,63
13:4	64

Ephesians	
2:12-22	60

Galatians	
4:6	27

Philippians	
3:21	112

Hebrews	
5:1-5	60
6:19-20	97
6:20	109
7:25	54,55
9:7	57
11:5-6	113

James	
5:16-18	16,39-40,52,55

Revelation	
11:3-13	110-112
12:1	89